Ordinary People, Remarkable Lives

Ordinary People, Remarkable Lives

Glenn Martin

G.P. Martin Publishing

Published 2025 by G.P. Martin Publishing

Website: www.glennmartin.com.au

Contact: info@glennmartin.com.au

Book layout and design by the author

Typeset in Sitka 11 pt

Printed by Lulu.com

V06092025

Cover images and design by the author.

ISBN: 978 0 6459543 7 1 (pbk.)

Table of Contents

List of Images

1 Introduction

The stories in this book come from the family history of Glenn Martin. The stories grew out of nothing. I had no knowledge of any of these people until I started diving into the family history, generation by generation. From all sorts of sources, not just certificates of births, deaths and marriages, facts emerged and people took shape, interesting people.

None of the family members in this book could claim to be a prominent public figure or in command of wealth. The point about the stories is that the people were ordinary citizens of society who were trying to get through the day, earning enough money to secure a home and feed their children, and endeavouring to be competent in their work. They are not saints, but they were true to that common endeavour of ordinary people, and in the process, they managed to live remarkable lives.

The range of the stories may be indicated by the birth dates and birthplaces of the main character in each story:

- Sarah Crosby in "Convict meets convict", was born 1831 at Waterford, Ireland
- William Archer in "The Duke of Edinburgh", was born 1813 at Harpenden, Hertfordshire, England
- Gordon Fink in "Gordon Fink and Gallipoli", was born 1884 in Melbourne
- Siegfried Hottelmann in "Love in wartime", was born 1911 at Holzminden, Germany
- Betsy Balcombe in "Betsy Balcombe and Napoleon at St Helena", was born 1802 at Clerkenwell, Middlesex, England
- Thomas Martin in "Thomas Martin and the Bethanga goldmine", was born 1834 at Towednack, Cornwall

- Ellen Welch in "The coalminer's daughter", was born 1822 at Balgonie Furnace, Fife, Scotland
- Robert Bridges in "The romance", was born 1719 at Kilconquhar, Fife, Scotland.

The stories are in no particular order, by theme, length, historical period or dramatic thrust. To me, they are all worthy stories to be told. The order probably reflects the order in which I wrote the stories. I will say that the stories are all stories that I have uncovered. They were not known to anyone before I started digging. Of course, in some cases, aspects of the stories were known. For example, Betsy's encounter with Napoleon has been a prolific source of new books (in the 1900s and 2000s), and Betsy herself wrote a book about it. But I have set out the many family links between Betsy and myself, and the links are a rich source of curious discoveries.

The background drama to all of these stories was the migration of my direct ancestors from the British Isles (England, Scotland and Ireland) to Australia in the nineteenth century: alone, in couples, and with entire families. This all occurred between the years 1838 and 1860, in my great great grandparents' generation.

Of the people mentioned above, several were immigrants to Australia: Sarah Crosby, Willliam Archer, Siegfried Hottelmann, Thomas Martin and Ellen Welch. And yes, there were convicts: Sarah Crosby, her husband, Edward Lewis, and William Archer. What occupations did the characters in these stories pursue?

- Sarah Crosby: house maid, mother
- William Archer: groom, farmer, fruit grower, fruit merchant, publican
- Gordon Fink: solicitor, soldier
- Siegfried Hottelmann: Baron, sailor
- Betsy Balcombe, music teacher, mother, author

- Thomas Martin: tin miner, stationary engine driver, miller, goldminer, manager of goldmine
- Ellen Welch: domestic servant, mother.
- Robert Bridges: baxter (baker).

Why these stories? Each one of these stories inspired me. We don't always land in benign circumstances, and it is a question of how we respond that matters. What I see in the stories is the striving to continue, to maintain one's spirit, and to create something of value: for oneself, for one's family, and for one's community.

In the midst of the travails of these people, there were great sadnesses, bold ventures, love, gratifying successes, and indomitable resilience. Looking at it all you might say, there is something admirable here, something admirable about these ordinary humans.

An introduction to the stories

Convict meets convict

Edward Lewis was a child convict, sent to Van Diemen's Land in 1846 for pickpocketing in London. Sarah Crosby came four years later, Irish, but transported for assaulting a policeman in an act of desperation as a homeless girl in London. The lives of convicts are quite constrained, so how did they meet? I followed their periods of confinement, and I have reached a conclusion about how they met. They were married in Hobart in May 1853.

The Duke of Edinburgh

The Duke of Edinburgh here refers to a hotel, one that was named after the duke, one of Queen Victoria's sons. Willliam Archer founded it at Pyrmont in the 1880s, and became the publican. The story is based on an interview I did with a second cousin of mine, Graeme Brennan. I was exploring another of my mother's stories, which associated the hotel with a white horse.

Gordon Fink and Gallipoli

Remarkably, perhaps, few people in my family have been in the armed forces. Gordon Fink married Alice Mackie, one of my first cousins, twice removed. He was a solicitor who had completed his training in Melbourne but who was on sabbatical from home. He met Alice in Sydney and they married. But their marriage was subsequently annulled, under pressure from Gordon's father, using false evidence. It was following this that Gordon joined the army and ended up at Gallipoli, where he died heroically.

Love in wartime

This story is now a book: *The Sailor, the Baron and the Dressmaker*, but I give the short-story version here. Siegfried Hottelmann arrived in Australia as a sailor, met Ellen Royall, one of my father's cousins, and they were married six weeks later. It was July 1939, and he was German, so after World War II was declared, he was sent to an internment camp in Victoria. Ellen followed him. It was there that she learned that back in Germany he had been a Baron. But Siegfried was a man of many adventures.

Betsy Balcombe and Napoleon

I have a family link with a girl who had a feisty but friendly relationship with Napoleon. Betsy Balcombe was the daughter of the merchant who was responsible for provisioning the party of Napoleon when he was in his final exile on the island of St Helena, in the Indian Ocean. Her relationship with him was the defining period of her life. The link between Betsy and myself is long and convoluted, but peppered with interesting people, such as the Mayor of Melbourne, and Australia's first international tennis player.

Thomas Martin and the Bethanga Goldmine

Thomas Martin had been a tin miner in Cornwall, but he left as a young man for South Australia. He was a miller, then a goldminer, and an early operator of steam engines. He spent two decades exploring gold sites in Victoria and New South Wales, finally becoming the manager of a goldmine at Bethanga in northern Victoria. He solved the problem of how to economically extract gold from quartz, after everyone else had failed. He was also a much loved and respected man, known as "the father of Bethanga".

The coalminer's daughter

Ellen Welch was a daughter of the manager of the coalmine at Balgonie Furnace, Fife. The family had been in the district for generations, and coalmining had been carried on here for hundreds of years. But Ellen, the fifth of six children, left home alone at sixteen and went to Australia as a single female. She married William Archer, a convict, and they had eight children. But there was a secret she kept for a lifetime.

The romance

This piece started as a story I heard from my mother when I was young. I always felt it was a bit mythological, but at the same time I thought there was a grain of truth in it. I wrote about it in *All the Rivers Come Together* (2022), when I thought it was a story that William Archer and Ellen Welch had made up to camouflage the fact that he had been a convict. Later, I thought there had to be something more to the story, and that that was to be found back in Scotland. I believe I have found the root of it, in the minutes of a meeting of a parish church council in 1749. Hence the story is called "An old story and an older one".

I have inherited these lives, the remarkable lives of ordinary people.

Image 1.1: Church and graveyard at Pittenweem, Fife, Scotland (Author, 2025)

2 Convict meets convict: Sarah Crosby and Edward Lewis

Preamble

Sarah Crosby and Edward Lewis (great great grandparents of mine) were both convicts in Van Diemen's Land. They met in Hobart and married. I have wondered how they met. In *All the Rivers Come Together* (2022), I wrote two stories describing Edward's convict servitude in Van Diemen's Land: "Edward Lewis at Point Puer", pp. 175-182, and "Edward Lewis: Grounds for intercession", pp. 183-186. Another story in the book dealt with the events surrounding the crime that Sarah committed in London that led to her sentence of transportation: "Sarah Crosby: A desperate spinster", pp. 187-194.

There is also a much larger work, *The Search for Edward Lewis* (2018), which addresses the whole of Edward's and Sarah's lives. The story below reflects particular things I have learned since writing these earlier works.

The story

Sarah Crosby and Edward Lewis are one set of my great great grandparents: my father's mother's mother's parents. Sarah and Edward were married in Hobart in the Roman Catholic Church of St Joseph in March 1853. Given that all my other great great grandparents are Protestant, and Edward Lewis was also Protestant, who was Sarah and how did she and Edward meet?

Sarah was Irish, so it makes sense that Sarah was Roman Catholic, while Edward (who was English) was Protestant. Sarah was most probably nineteen, and Edward was twenty-three, when they married. When did they arrive in Hobart? Van Diemen's Land had started in 1803 as a convict colony, but by the 1840s the government was interested in gaining free settlers.

But Sarah and Edward were not free settlers; they would have been a bit young for that anyway. Edward arrived first, in 1846, when he was only sixteen. And Sarah arrived in 1850, at the age of either sixteen or eighteen (there is a lack of clarity in the records). While the government was making efforts to attract free settlers, it was still a convict colony and as such it was unattractive to most would-be settlers from Great Britain.

In 1851 the Colonial Land and Emigration Commission sent out two shiploads of Irish female migrants to address the imbalance of males and females in the colony.[1] This was the first such venture by the government. Transportation of convicts to Van Diemen's Land ended in 1853. Sarah was one of the last female convicts to be sent here.

Edward had been a pickpocket in London and he had been caught stealing a purse and ten shillings from a lady at Kensington. He was transported for ten years, arriving on the *Lady Palmyra* in August 1846. He was sent to Point Puer.[2] It was a recently established boys' prison, adjacent to the large men's penal settlement at Port Arthur. It was intended

---

[1] Libraries Tasmania, "Free Immigration to Tasmania 1803-1946", link.
[2] Edward Lewis, No. 18862, *Palmyra*, 1846, Assignment Lists and Associated Papers, CON13/1/13, images 80, 81, Tasmanian Names Index; Edward Lewis, No. 18862, *Palmyra*, 1846, Indents of Male Convicts, CON14/1/36, image 16, Tasmanian Names Index.

that boys would learn a trade so they could pursue an honest life when they were released.[3]

Sarah, the Irish girl, had left Ireland, probably on her own, perhaps fleeing, during the potato famine (1846-1850). She was born in Waterford and I do not know the fate of her parents. She worked as a servant in a house in Bath for a while (as many Irish did), but she ended up in London.[4] She might have come to London to try and contact her brother, James, who may have been heading for America. She would have connected with other Irish people in London. She had one encounter with the police, the charge being drunkenness, and she was locked up for three days.[5] However, it is possible that this incident happened in Bath; perhaps she was dismissed by her employer because of it.

On 31 January 1849, around eight in the evening, a policeman "moved her on" (his words) from the Refuge for the Houseless Poor in Whitecross Street, London. The evidence submitted at court was that she had been noisy and used bad language. I imagine her hungry, cold, afraid, and despairing. It was not uncommon for people to freeze to death in winter on the streets of London at this time.[6] She lashed out at the policeman, who had been joined by another policeman, and they were attempting to subdue her when she took a small knife from her bag and stabbed one of them in the arm.

---

[3] Nunn, Cameron, '"Making Them Good and Useful": The Ideology of Juvenile Penal Reformation at Carters' Barracks and Point Puer', *History Australia*, vol. 14, no. 3, 2017, pp. 329-343.
[4] Sarah Crosby, Convict No. 1031, *St Vincent*, 1850, Conduct register of female convicts arriving in the period of the probation system, Tasmanian Archives, CON41.
[5] Sarah Crosby, Conduct register of female convicts.
[6] Mayhew, Henry, *London Labour and the London Poor*, Volume 1 of 4, Griffin, Bohn & Co., London, 1851.

The newspaper articles on the trial described her as "A Desperate Spinster".[7] She was sentenced to seven years in Van Diemen's Land; the magistrate described her as a "fit and proper subject for the colonies".[8] She was sent to Millbank Prison on 26 February 1849. However, Millbank was an unhealthy place, and it had an outbreak of cholera in 1849.[9] Despite this, Sarah survived.

Sarah is the only female convict in the convict lists for Australia who was transported for cutting and wounding a policeman. There were ten males who had been found guilty of assaulting a policeman; they were given sentences from fourteen years to life.[10] Notably, never again in her life did Sarah stab a person. She was in an extreme situation where she felt her very life to be in danger.

Sarah Crosby's voyage to Australia on the *St Vincent* took 106 days.[11] She spent most of that time in the infirmary, two bouts of about five weeks each, with rheumatism, constipation, and vomiting of blood.[12] When the ship arrived

---

[7] *Lloyd's Weekly London*, Newspaper, 11 March 1849, p. 4, British Newspaper Archive, accessed 22 October 2015.

[8] Sarah Crosby, Proceedings of Central Criminal Court, 26 February 1849, p. 109, https://www.oldbaileyonline.org , accessed 22 October 2015.

[9] Johanna Lemon and Peter Daniel, Millbank Prison, http://www.choleraandthethames.co.uk/cholera-in-london/cholera-in-westminster/millbank-prison accessed 1 July 2015.

[10] Search on convicts convicted of cutting and wounding a policeman, https://convictrecords.com.au/crimes/cutting-and-wounding-a-policeman , 16 May 2022.

[11] Shipping Intelligence, *Britannia and Trades' Advocate*, 11 Apr 1850, p. 3, http://nla.gov.au/nla.news-article226533531. accessed 11 May 2022. Note, various newspaper reports give different departure dates. I accept 19 December 1849, from the convict records.

[12] Sicknesses of Sarah Crosby, Surgeon's Journal (Dr Samuel Donnelly), *St Vincent*, 7 December 1849 to 17 April 1850, pp. 5-6,

at Hobart on 4 April 1850, Sarah, one of 205 female convicts, was said to be very much improved, and she was discharged.

I had thought that Sarah was sent to Cascades Female Factory (south of Hobart) on her arrival. That had been the practice during the early days of the colony, and up to the 1840s. From 1844, female convicts spent up to six months in "reformation and training" on the probation ship *Anson* in Hobart before they were sent out for employment. However, the *Anson* was closed down in early 1850, before Sarah arrived.[13] Newspaper reports and other sources show that convicts from the *St Vincent* were hired directly off the ship.[14]

The next clue to Sarah's circumstances comes from her indent (her convict record). It notes an incident that occurred on 29 June 1850, and her employer's name is given as 'Sutton'.[15] This was Charles Sutton, an inn-keeper at Oatlands.[16] So, Sarah, a young Irish girl (who was either eighteen or twenty, with black hair, hazel eyes, pale

---

9-10, https://www.femaleconvicts.org.au/docs/ships/StVincent1850_SJ2.pdf , accessed 3 May 2022.

[13] Alexander, Alison (ed.), *Repression, Reform and Resilience: A History of the Cascades Female Factory*, Convict Women's Press, Hobart, 2016, Chapter 9, "The Probation System", pp.121-137; P.R. Eldershaw, *Guide to the Public Records of Tasmania*, Section 3: Convict Department, Archives Office of Tasmania, Hobart, 2003.

[14] Local, *Hobart Town Advertiser*, 9 April 1850, p. 3, http://nla.gov.au/nla.news-article264606531, accessed 11 May 2022; Joan Goodrick, *Life in Old Van Diemens Land*, Rigby, Melbourne, 1977, p. 83.

[15] Sarah Crosby, Convict No. 1031, *St Vincent*, 1850, Conduct register of female convicts arriving in the period of the probation system, Tasmanian Archives, CON41.

[16] Census record for Charles Sutton, Oatlands, 1848, Van Diemen's Land Census, Tasmanian Names Index, CEN1/1/94, accessed 12 May 2022.

complexion, 5' 1 ¾" tall (1570 mm)) was employed as a servant in a small town midway between Hobart and Launceston. The town had started life in the 1820s as a garrison town for police and convicts.[17] To arrive there must have been a huge shock to her, after her experiences with the potato famine in Ireland, being homeless in London, the incident at the refuge, and being very sick on the voyage to Australia.

The incident at Oatlands was that Sarah was "found with a man in her bed room" after 9:30 at night.[18] She was dismissed from service, and sent to Cascades Female Factory in Hobart as punishment. We learn this from her convict indent. But what else can we learn? Who was Charles Sutton, what was the name of the inn, and who was the man in her bedroom?

Charles Sutton was born in London in about 1800. He was a butcher by trade. He was tried for burglary in 1819 with two other men, and transported to Van Diemen's Land for seven years. He came out on the *Dromedary*. He received his Ticket of Leave in 1826.[19] He married Sarah Wright in June 1827 at Hobart. She could read and write; he couldn't (the marriage register shows her signature, but just an 'X' for his mark).[20]

I am not sure what Charles Sutton did to obtain the funds for it, but he began to purchase parcels of land, first at Ross, then at Oatlands. It is possible the money came from his wife's family. Sutton took over the Wilmot Arms hotel in

---

[17] Sarah Crosby, Convict conduct record.
[18] This was not uncommon. See Babette Smith, *Defiant Voices*, NLA Publishing, Canberra, 2021, p. 128.
[19] Charles Sutton, convict no. 184, *Dromedary*, 1819, conduct register, Tasmanian Archives, CON31-1-38 image 66.
[20] Marriage register entry of Charles Sutton and Sarah Wright, married 6 June 1827, Register of Marriages in Hobart, Tasmanian Archives. RGD36/1/1 No. 1004.

Oatlands in 1850. It had previously been called the Franklin Hotel, but its name had been changed in 1844 when the new Lieut.-Governor, Sir John Eardly-Wilmot, arrived in the colony.

The employment of Sarah Crosby off the *St Vincent* must have been part of Sutton's initial efforts to staff his hotel. Her job was 'chamber-maid'. Perhaps it was in her favour that she had worked as a servant in Bath (one assumes, at one of the great houses).

Is it possible to conjecture who the man in Sarah Crosby's bedroom was? There are several possibilities. It is possible that Charles Sutton was the man in her bedroom. It was not uncommon in the convict days for the employer of female convicts (who were mostly domestic servants) to engage in sex with them; if the employer wished to do this, the convict had little choice in the matter.

One author has pointed out that male convicts generally worked outside of homes, on roads, fences, timber-getting, and tending animals, while women convicts generally worked indoors, so they were always in close proximity to their employers. There was more opportunity for sexual incidents to occur.[21] But one has to ask: who, then, made the charge against her? In some situations where the employer had been familiar with a female servant against her will, the servant refused to work, and bailed themselves out of the job, going back to Cascades willingly.

This did not happen here. Would Sarah have even known of that option? One could assume that the charge was put by Charles Sutton's wife. I think the fact that Sarah Sutton could read and write, and Charles couldn't, gave her some power in the relationship, especially having to deal with the daily affairs of a hotel business. If Charles had

---

[21] Babette Smith, 2021, *Defiant Voices*, NLA Publishing, Canberra, p. 125; Kay Daniels, 1998, *Convict Women*, Allen & Unwin, Sydney, p. 80.

interfered with Sarah Crosby, Sarah Sutton could have exercised her power.

However, this is not the only possibility. In 1831, Charles and Sarah Sutton had a son, also called Charles. In 1850 he would have been nineteen years old, so he was about the same age as Sarah Crosby. It is possible that he was the culprit, and his parents didn't want their son to form a relationship with a convict. And they may have chosen to blame her for the incident. Or perhaps Sarah Sutton was even acting to get Sarah Crosby out of a difficult situation.

The wording of the charge against Sarah is unfortunate (she was "found with a man in her bed room"), in that it infers that she orchestrated the event, whereas it seems unlikely that that was true. It is more likely that the male, whoever it was, was the instigator. And there is yet another person whom it could have been.

Remembering that Sarah was Irish, there was another Irish person in town: Kevin Izod O'Doherty. He was a Dubliner who had been studying to become a doctor when he became involved in the Young Ireland movement. They were rebels protesting against the presence of the British in Ireland, and their domination of civil life. They were active in the 1840s. Kevin was co-editor of the nationalist paper, the *Irish Tribune*. They published a number of anti-British articles.

In 1848 he was arrested and tried for treason-felony, and transported for ten years to Van Diemen's Land. Later, I learned that one of his compatriots, Thomas Francis Meagher, was actually arrested in Waterford (Sarah's home town). The rebels had been active in Waterford and had strong support from the local people.

Arriving in Hobart in October 1849, Kevin was immediately given a Ticket of Leave (as was the practice for

Irish rebels), and allowed to settle in the Oatlands district.[22] He was given lodgings at Elm Cottage by John Ryan, an Irishman who was a devoted Catholic. Could O'Doherty have come into contact with Sarah?

Elm Cottage was close to the Wilmot Arms, straight across the road and just twenty metres along. Not only this, but during 1850 a Roman Catholic church was being built in the town, and in the meantime, Mass was held on Sundays at Elm Cottage. Also, the Catholic priest was staying at the cottage while the presbytery was being built.[23] One assumes that Sarah Crosby took the opportunity to go to Mass and meet with some fellow Irish folk.

There are reasons against Kevin O'Doherty and Sarah Crosby having a liaison. He was about ten years older than her (not a compelling reason). He was educated while she could neither read nor write. He was a devout Catholic, and he had a fiancée waiting for him in Dublin, Mary Eva Kelly.[24] (He married her in London in 1855.) But Sarah was Irish (they even had Waterford in common), she was young, and imagine if she were also beautiful?

Of course, the culprit in Sarah's bedroom could have been someone else entirely. Yet, one normally gives primary consideration to those who are known and who have opportunity.

There is another, relevant fact. On 27 April 1851, Sarah gave birth to a baby girl; the baby was called Mary

[22] Kevin Ozod O'Doherty, Australian Dictionary of Biography, https://adb.anu.edu.au/biography/odoherty-kevin-izod-4319 Accessed 16 May 2022.
[23] From plaque outside Elm Cottage, High Street, Oatlands.
[24] Ross & Heather Patrick, 1989, *Exiles Undaunted: The Irish Rebels Kevin and Eva O'Doherty*, University of Queensland Press, Brisbane.

Ann.[25] That makes early to mid-August 1850 the likely time of conception. So, the episode at the end of June was not the occasion of conception, if, indeed, intercourse occurred. Note, the charge against Sarah was that there was a man in her bedroom, not that he was in her bed. True, this could have simply been a euphemism, but perhaps the man's mere presence in her room was sufficient to have her dismissed.

Yet there is more to the story. In August 1850, O'Doherty was allowed to move to Hobart, where he took up work as a surgeon at St Mary's Hospital at 38 Davey St. It was a convict hospital from 1847 to 1860. He attracted much respect among the Irish prisoners, who called him "St Kevin". O'Doherty had previously had experience as a doctor working in a hospital in Dublin during the potato famine.[26]

It is a long shot, but a case could be made that Kevin O'Doherty was besotted with Sarah and contrived to be allowed to go to Hobart, and he met up with Sarah there and was the father of her child. It is noted that the account by Ross and Heather Patrick (1989), emphasises Kevin's unfailing attachment to his fiancé in Ireland, Eva Kelly.

That was the last Sarah was to see of Oatlands, although she would have passed through a few years later when she and Edward Lewis moved up to Launceston to live (1855). Sarah was sent to Cascades from Oatlands, but she did not stay there for long, suggesting that Cascades was not punishing her for a supposed crime or infraction.

Almost immediately she was sent out again, to be a servant at the Police Magistrates Office (PMO) in Hobart. This was in the same building as the Court House, located

---

[25] Birth register entry of Mary Ann Crosby, born 27 April 1851, Register of Births in Hobart, Tasmanian Archives, RGD33/1/4, No. 364.
[26] Kevin Ozod O'Doherty, Dictionary of Irish Biography, https://www.dib.ie/biography/odoherty-kevin-izod-a6680 Accessed 25 January 2024.

on the corner of Murray and Macquarie Streets, just one block away from St Mary's Hospital.[27] She was likely there in August 1850. Accordingly, someone at the PMO could have been the father of her child, or somebody stationed close by, namely, Dr O'Doherty.

Sarah was married to Edward Lewis on 7 March 1853, at the Roman Catholic Church of St Joseph in Davey Street, Hobart.[28] Edward had served most of his time as a convict at Point Puer, but it was shut down in March 1849, following which he was sent to the Prisoner Barracks in Hobart, probably as a clerk, for he could read and write. The Prisoner Barracks was in Campbell Street. It had been constructed to house men waiting to be assigned to free settlers, and to house men who were in government employment. It housed over 600 convicts.

August 1850 was also the month when Edward obtained his Ticket of Leave (on 20th). A ticket of leave freed a convict to work for wages and to live independently. Edward graduated from being a convict to becoming a special constable in the police force.[29] As a special constable, he could have been stationed at numerous locations around town, or at just one. Given his ability to read and write, he

---

[27] Sarah Crosby, Convict conduct record; map of Hobart Town: Plan of layout of streets of Hobart, 1825?, Hobart Maps, Lands and Surveys Department, Tasmanian Archives, AF394/1/10; Smith, Augustus Frederick, Military sketch of Hobart Town, 1847-1855?, Publisher: Hobart?, NSW State Library, Record Identifier 74VvaOROp7m3.
[28] Marriage register entry of Edward Lewis and Sarah Crosby, married 7 March 1853, Register of Marriages in Hobart, Tasmanian Archives. RGD37/1/12 No. 683.
[29] Noted in marriage register entry for Edward Lewis and Sarah Crosby.

could have been used as a clerk at the PMO.[30] This opens the possibility that he was brought directly into a sphere where Sarah was working.

Another possibility is that Edward was stationed at the Cascades Female Factory. Sarah spent numerous periods of time there between her stints with employers. What would Edward have been doing there as a policeman? He would not have been policing the inmates; the police were only called to do that if there was a serious incident, like a rebellion or a riot (which had happened more than once!).

The Factory employed two policemen whose job it was to convey messages to and from police headquarters in Hobart. They were always on call. The room where they stayed was part of the Matron's Cottage but cut off from it. They had their own separate entrance onto the street, because the policemen were forbidden from having any interaction with the female convicts.[31]

However, the reality of life under the convict system was seldom as strict as the authorities wanted it to be. One can imagine, in this scenario, that opportunity arose for Edward to encounter Sarah.

There is no evidence that Edward was the father of Sarah's child, and a woman having a child with no named father was not unusual at the time. On the page in the Births Register for the birth of Mary Ann Crosby, four out of ten mothers had a child with no named father.[32] It was a symptom of the times. Hobart was a bustling town, but Van

---

[30] Stefan Petrow, Policing in a Penal Colony: Governor Arthur's Police System in Van Diemen's Land, 1826-1836, *Law and History Review*, Vol. 18, No. 2 (Summer, 2000), pp. 351-395.
[31] Plaque at Matron's Cottage at Cascades Female Factory, 16 Delgraves St, South Hobart, visited 23 August 2023.
[32] Birth register entry of Mary Ann Crosby, born 27 April 1851.

Diemen's Land was still a convict colony, and the imbalance of male and female numbers was still pronounced.[33]

I had at first assumed that Sarah was at Cascades when her baby was born. A new nursery for mothers and babies had been built at Cascades, which opened in mid-1850. Its first occupants were mothers and babies from a ship arriving from England, the *Baretto Junior*, in July. However, the Convict Department still had a lease on a house in south Hobart, Dynnyrne House, where convict mothers and babies were kept, and the lease on the house did not expire until 1851.

Women and children who were already in the colony remained at Dynnyrne House. It was grossly overcrowded: "the building was so crowded that it was 'not... possible to maintain order and cleanliness'".[34] After it was closed, the women and children did not go to Cascades; they were sent to other places, such as Brickfields in north Hobart. It was not until April 1854 that they were sent back to Cascades.[35] Despite this, Sarah was back at Cascades by January 1852 (see later).

Under the convict system, women kept their babies with them for six months while they were breast-feeding. After that, the babies were weaned and separated from their mothers, and sent to the Queen's Orphanage, while the women were sent out to employers again. The system did barbaric things to women and children, while the authorities persuaded themselves that they were doing the

---

[33] James Barnard, Statistics of Van Diemen's Land for 1849, 1852, https://eprints.utas.edu.au/17727/1/1852_I._Barnard_Observatio ns_on_the_Statistics_of_Van_Diemen%27s_Land.pdf, accessed 16 May 2022.
[34] Kippen, Rebecca, 2006, 'And the Mortality Frightful': Infant and Child Mortality in the Convict Nurseries of Van Diemen's Land, Demography and Sociology Program, Australian National University, p. 7.
[35] Kippen, 2006, p. 7.

right (ie the righteous) thing. The underlying intent was punishment, mixed up with unsavoury beliefs about convict women being depraved, and who would bring their children up to be the same.

A doctor came out from England in 1854 to be the medical officer at Cascades: Dr Edward Hall. He was so appalled by the conditions there that he began to investigate its history, and he documented the situation as part of his making an impassioned protest to the government about it. He showed that mortality in the nursery in 1851, 1852 and 1853 was around four times higher than mortality of children of a similar age in the general Hobart district. He calculated death rates under the age of three to be around 40 per cent.[36]

I suspect that Sarah's baby died.[37] There is no record of the baby's death, and there is also no record of any later life for her (eg at the Queen's Orphanage). Sarah was sent out to other employers.[38]

The convict indent shows that Sarah had three run-ins with Mrs Hodgins, the assistant matron, for disorderly conduct, during the period January to June 1852.[39] I wonder if this was related to something that was happening with her baby, if the baby was still alive, or whether she was experiencing grief after the child's death, or whether she was changing her view of herself now that she had become a mother, to want to stand up for herself. And, was it also related to the influence of her social context, being among the other female convicts? Alternatively, was she already in

---

[36] Kippen, 2006, p. 8.
[37] Lucy Frost, "The convict nurseries", in Alison Alexander (ed.), *Repression, Reform and Resilience: A History of the Cascades Female Factory*, Convict Women's Press, 2016, pp. 138-151.
[38] Lucy Frost, *Footsteps and Voices*, Female Factory Historic Site, Hobart, 2004; Babette Smith, *Defiant Voices*, pp. 220-239.
[39] Sarah Crosby, Convict conduct record.

a relationship with Edward? If she were to marry him, she would be free to leave Cascades under his 'supervision'.

Sarah had numerous employers after Charles Sutton and the stint at the PMO. They were all for short periods of time. There was Stephen Hughes, postmaster and schoolmaster at O'Brien's Bridge (November 1850), Will Sweeney (August 1852) at Carupol(?) Station, Thomas Terry (September 1852), miller at New Norfolk, Mr Rowbottom (September 1852), New Norfolk. On 9 November 1852 she was granted a Ticket of Leave, with the condition: "Not to reside in Hobart Town".[40] However, I noted that this condition seems to have been widely ignored.

On 21 January 1853, just a couple of months after receiving her ticket of leave, Sarah was given permission to marry Edward Lewis.[41] After their marriage in March, they lived in Watchorn Street, Hobart. The first children of the marriage were born there: twin girls, Sarah Ann and Mary Susannah (12 May 1854).[42] The family moved to Launceston and the next child, Edmond, was born there (1855). My great grandmother, Ellen Elizabeth (1857), was next.[43] There was one more child, Margaret (1860), and afterwards, two children who died soon after birth.

The family moved to Sydney. Sarah and Edward lived what appears to be an unsettled life, and they may have separated. Sarah died at Annandale on 4 September 1897, in a house she was purchasing. Her death certificate says she was sixty-four (thus, born May 1833, but the early records

---

[40] Sarah Crosby, Convict conduct record.
[41] Sarah Crosby, Convict conduct record.
[42] Birth register entries for Sarah Ann and Mary Susannah Lewis, born 12 May 1854, Register of Births in Hobart, Tasmanian Archives, RGD33/1/5, No. 980, 981.
[43] Birth register entry for Ellen Elizabeth Lewis, born 24 October 1857, Register of Births in Launceston, Tasmanian Archives, RGD33/1/35, No. 1251.

are not consistent; it may have been 1831).[44] Her gravestone at Rookwood says (proudly): "In Memory of Sarah Anne Lewis, Native of County Waterford, Ireland".[45] Strangely, the death of Edward Lewis is unknown. I have been unable to find a death certificate for him, a report of his death, or a grave. From scraps of evidence I have gleaned, I believe he died around the same time as Sarah.

References

Primary sources

1841 England Census, The National Archives, England, HO107/698/13, UK Census Collection.

Assignment Lists and Associated Papers, CON13/1/13, Tasmanian Names Index.

Britannia and Trades' Advocate.

Conduct register of female convicts arriving in the period of the probation system, Tasmanian Archives, CON41.

Headstone of Sarah Anne Lewis (nee Crosby), Rookwood Necropolis.

Hobart Town Advertiser.

Indents of Male Convicts, CON14/1/36, Tasmanian Names Index.

James Barnard, Statistics of Van Diemen's Land for 1849, 1852, https://eprints.utas.edu.au/17727/1/1852 I. Barnard Observatio ns on the Statistics of Van Diemen%27s Land.pdf

Lloyd's Weekly London.

---

[44] Death certificate for Sarah Lewis.
[45] Headstone of Sarah Anne Lewis (nee Crosby), died 4 September 1897, Annandale (Sydney), Rookwood Necropolis, sighted, 1 October 2016.

Map of Hobart Town: Plan of layout of streets of Hobart, 1825?, Hobart Maps, Lands and Surveys Department, Tasmanian Archives, AF394/1/10.

NRS-13660-4-577-Series 4_14206, Probate Packets, New South Wales State Archives & Records.

Proceedings of Central Criminal Court, 26 February 1849, p. 109, https://www.oldbaileyonline.org

Registry of Births, Deaths & Marriages, New South Wales.

Smith, Augustus Frederick, Military sketch of Hobart Town, 1847-1855?, Publisher: Hobart?, NSW State Library, Record Identifier 74VvaOROp7m3.

Surgeon's Journal (Dr Samuel Donnelly), *St Vincent*, 1850.

Tasmanian Archives, Registers of Births in Hobart, RGD33.

Tasmanian Archives, Registers of Births in Launceston, RGD33.

Tasmanian Archives, Registers of Marriages in Hobart, RGD37.

Van Diemen's Land Census, Tasmanian Names Index, CEN1/1/94.

Secondary sources

Alexander, Alison (ed.), Repression, Reform and Resilience: A History of the Cascades Female Factory, Convict Women's Press, Hobart, 2016.

Eldershaw, P.R., *Guide to the Public Records of Tasmania*, Section 3: Convict Department, Archives Office of Tasmania, Hobart, 2003.

Frost, Lucy, *Footsteps and Voices*, Female Factory Historic Site, Hobart, 2004.

Goodrick, Joan, *Life in Old Van Diemens Land*, Rigby, Melbourne, 1977.

Kippen, Rebecca, 2006, 'And the Mortality Frightful': Infant and Child Mortality in the Convict Nurseries of Van Diemen's Land, Demography and Sociology Program, Australian National University.

Nunn, Cameron, '"Making Them Good and Useful": The Ideology of Juvenile Penal Reformation at Carters' Barracks and Point Puer', *History Australia*, vol. 14, no. 3, 2017, pp. 329–343.

Petrow, Stefan, Policing in a Penal Colony: Governor Arthur's Police System in Van Diemen's Land, 1826-1836, *Law and History Review*, Vol. 18, No. 2 (Summer, 2000), pp. 351-395.

Smith, Babette, *Defiant Voices*, NLA Publishing, Canberra, 2021.

Image 2.1: Irish potato famine: scene at the gate of the workhouse (Wikimedia Commons)

3 A convict, a hotel and a white horse

William Archer, my great great grandfather (on my mother's side), was a convict. He was transported to Australia in 1838 for the theft of twenty-eight pairs of high shoes, and the basket that contained them. However, later in life he became a publican, and he established the Duke of Edinburgh Hotel at Pyrmont in Sydney. I gradually unearthed this story, having been told initially by my mother, "There are no convicts in our family."

I interviewed my second cousin, Graeme Brennan.[46] We have the same great grandfather, James Archer, who is a son of William Archer. Graeme grew up knowing about the hotel, and knowing his grandmother, Dolly Archer, who married John Patrick Brennan. Dolly (christened Alice Lillian Archer) was my grandfather's youngest sister. If the Brennans were in the car together and driving past the hotel, Dolly would point up to one of the first-floor windows and declare, "That was my bedroom. I was born in that hotel."[47]

My mother knew about the hotel and told us children, although she didn't know much more than that it was the Duke of Edinburgh Hotel, and it had been at Pyrmont. Later in life she said it was in the Archer family for a long time, and it was demolished in the 1980s when Darling Harbour was rebuilt. There was a white horse at the hotel, and the Archers bought a hotel at Windsor and took the horse with them. (My mother died in 2017 at the age of ninety-three.) My investigations established that the hotel still exists at

---

[46] Graeme Brennan, interview by Glenn Martin, digital audio recording, Cooranbong NSW, 18 March 2022, original held by interviewer.
[47] Graeme Brennan, interview by Glenn Martin.

Pyrmont, although it has a new name: the Harlequin Inn. I couldn't find anything about an Archer hotel at Windsor.

Graeme Brennan was the key. He told me his life story, which started with working for the Rural Bank and working part-time in hotels. Eventually he left the bank and became a publican. He went into partnership with a man called Bourne, and they bought the Quarrymans Hotel at Pyrmont, which is about 200 metres down Harris Street from the Duke of Edinburgh.

Graeme said many publicans were friends, and visited each other's hotels. One time, the publican of the Duke wanted to go on holidays to Melbourne, and he asked Graeme to look after his hotel for him, which he did. Soon after this, Graeme and Bourne decided to sell the Quarrymans and buy a hotel freehold out near Windsor – the Tourmaline, which was the name of a racehorse. And it had a huge statue of a horse outside, reared up on its hind legs.

I told Graeme what my mother had said and he laughed. He said it was easy for stories to become garbled. After thinking about it some more, he said, "No, there never was a white horse connected with the Duke of Edinburgh Hotel." The most he could offer was that the statue at the Tourmaline needed repairs, and for three months it was undercoated white, before the painter painted it all silver. That seems somewhat of a stretch for my mother's story.

However, Graeme was born in 1947, and he was talking about the time around 1980. My mother was talking about when she was young, say, around 1930.

The next question was, how did my mother know what she told me? Who told her? But I realised it was because she knew Dolly, who was her aunt (I have a picture of them in the same photo). Dolly's elder brother, Thomas Richard Archer, was my mother's father. At the rare family gatherings that occurred, mostly for weddings or funerals, my mother would talk with Aunt Dolly, and what Aunt Dolly said turned into what my mother heard and tried to make sense of, and so I got the story that I did.

However, the idea of the white horse has not gone away, even though I can now guess how my mother got her story muddled. She was also wrong about the hotel being demolished, but it's true that it disappeared when Darling Harbour was remodelled, because its name was changed.

My mother was wrong about the hotel remaining in the family for so long. Graeme said that James Archer took over the hotel from his father William, then lost it all because he was a drunkard. I had established, through the City of Sydney Archives, that the Archer family lost ownership in the early 1900s.[48] The Scottish Australian Investment Company took over as owner before 1910. I figured this wasn't the family, and I was right. It was a company set up by a group of businessmen in Scotland in the 1840s(!) to buy properties in Australia for investment purposes.[49] It was profitable over a long period of time.

Why was the idea of the white horse still alive? For Graeme and myself, it was for different reasons, but in both cases it went back to England, where William Archer came from. Graeme knew the basic facts, as did I, about William's experiences as a young man. He was born at Harpenden in Hertfordshire, and at the age of twenty-five he was convicted of stealing, and transported to New South Wales for seven years. He arrived in Sydney in February 1838 on

---

[48] Duke of Edinburgh Hotel, 150 Harris Street, *Sands Sydney, Suburban and Country Commercial Directory*, 1909, p. 72, City of Sydney Archives and History Resources, https://archives.cityofsydney.nsw.gov.au/nodes/view/1899870 Accessed 23 March 2022.
[49] Scottish Australian Investment Company, Australian National University Archives, https://archivescollection.anu.edu.au/index.php/scottish-australian-investment-company-limited Accessed 19 March 2022.

the *Waterloo* among 224 male convicts.[50] He was sent to the Hunter Valley, where he worked as a farmhand for the Australian Agricultural Company.[51]

William met a woman, an assisted migrant, Ellen Welch from Scotland, and they were married in July 1844. What Graeme noticed was that the marriage record stated the location as "Parish of Dungog, Eldon, Stroud, in the Counties of Gloucester and Durham, Uffington".[52] He had viewed the record through Ancestry.com. The print version I purchased from the Registry of Births, Deaths and Marriages (BDM) did not mention Uffington.[53]

Uffington is a parish, a unit of land division in the Maitland and Dungog areas of New South Wales.[54] But originally, it was the area in England associated with a white horse formed into the landscape (deep trenches filled with crushed white chalk), 110 metres long. It is called the

---

[50] William Archer, *Waterloo*, 1838, Convict Indents 1788-1842, Non-Annotated Printed Indentures, accessed from Ancestry.com, 21 March 2022.

[51] William Archer, served his sentence at Raymond Terrace on lands of the Australian Agricultural Company; *Waterloo*, 1838, Butts of Certificates of Freedom, 24 September 1844, New South Wales State Archives, NRS 12210. Accessed 10 October 2014.

[52] Marriage certificate of William Archer and Ellen Welch, married 15 July 1844; location: Dungog, Eldon, Stroud, Uffington, New South Wales, NSW Pioneer Index: Pioneer Series 1778 – 1888, Marriage Index 1788 – 1950, Ancestry.com, accessed 22 March 2022.

[53] Marriage certificate of William Archer and Ellen Welch, married 15 July 1844; location: Parish of Eldon & Dungog, in the Counties of Gloucester & Durham, Registry of Births, Deaths and Marriages, New South Wales (BDM), No. 541, Vol. 29.

[54] Map, Parish of Uffington, County of Durham: Land Districts of Maitland & Dungog, Port Stephens & Wallarobba Shires, Eastern Division NSW, Department of Lands, 1955, National Library of Australia, https://nla.gov.au/nla.obj-316238671/view Accessed 22 March 2022.

Uffington White Horse.[55] It predates the Romans, going back to Celtic times, and it may have had a ritual or religious purpose for worshippers of the horse-goddess Epona. There is more than one of these. On a trip to England in 2025, I went to Stonehenge, and this white horse was visible on the journey from Bath.

Graeme wondered why the area in the Hunter was given that name; that would have happened in the early 1800s. I do not know.

My association is different. I was looking at Harpenden on Google Maps, and started looking at the accompanying photos. One of them was of the White Horse Inn, which dates back to the 1600s. It is still operating.[56] It is on the outskirts of Harpenden. I could suggest that, since William was a groom in Harpenden, he could have worked at the White Horse Inn. True, but that does not explain how the white horse is associated with the hotel at Pyrmont. Nor does Graeme's connection of the Hunter Valley parish name with the Uffington White Horse explain its relevance to William Archer or the hotel.

Also, we have to accept that the hotel was named after the Duke of Edinburgh, not the white horse. The Duke of Edinburgh was Alfred, the second son of Queen Victoria, and in 1867 he made the first ever royal tour of Australia. He spent seven months in the colonies and was very popular.[57] There was an incident: he was shot in Sydney in March 1868 by a rebellious Irishman. The Irishman was hung; the Duke

---

[55] Uffington White Horse, Wikipedia, https://en.wikipedia.org/wiki/Uffington_White_Horse Accessed 21 March 2022. (I would argue this is an appropriate use of this source, for my purposes.)

[56] White Horse Inn, https://www.thewhitehorseharpenden.co.uk/

[57] Duke of Edinburgh, Australian Dictionary of Biography, http://adb.anu.edu.au/biography/edinburgh-duke-of-3467 Accessed 5 November 2016.

survived. The Duke's unfortunate injury and recovery cemented him in the people's affections. The Duke made two more visits to Australia – in 1869 and 1870. His visits prompted a plethora of hotels around Australia to be named after him. This is one theory: marketing opportunism.

William Archer's hotel dates from around 1880-1882.[58] But there is also another fact to consider. William and family had gone back to England in the late 1860s to live. They bought an orchard at Kent. However, in 1874, they returned to Australia to live, as did many colonists who returned to the "Mother Country".[59] Whilst living in England, they may have visited the Duke of Edinburgh Hotel at Brixton. It would have been on the way to London for them.[60] It was only fifteen miles away from their orchard in Kent. That's another theory: it was a private joke, or the basis of a good story.

The white horse is still an open question. After talking with Graeme Brennan, I still don't know the source of the story, but it is interesting that my mother told it. Perhaps it

---

[58] Duke of Edinburgh Hotel, corner Harris & Union Streets, *Sands Sydney, Suburban and Country Commercial Directory*, 1882, p. 64, City of Sydney Archives and History Resources, https://archives.cityofsydney.nsw.gov.au/nodes/view/495003 Accessed 21 June 2021.

[59] Census record for William Archer and family, Wilmington, Kent, 1871 England & Wales Census, UK Public Record Office, Ref. R.G. 10/886, accessed on My Heritage, 8 November 2021. Passenger list entries for William Archer and family, *St Osyth*, arriving Port Phillip, 25 December 1874 from London, Public Record Office of Victoria, Inward Overseas Passenger Lists, July-December 1874, British & Foreign Ports.

[60] The current building dates from 1937, but there was a previous building dating back to the 1860s. The Duke of Edinburgh Hotel, Historic England, https://historicengland.org.uk/listing/the-list/list-entry/1427801?section=official-list-entry Accessed 21 March 2022.

goes back to William Archer. I am convinced he liked a good story.

Image 3.1: The Duke of Edinburgh Hotel, ~1900 (Graeme Brennan)

Image 3.2: Duke of Edinburgh Hotel, 1949 (Tooth & Co., brewery)

4 Gallipoli: The end of a fraught life

This essay was originally written for the unit "HAA107 Families and War" in the Diploma of Family History at the University of Tasmania, 2022. The assignment topic was "Biography of a First World War Soldier".

"War assumes a prominent place in Australia's awareness of history."
Professor Peter Stanley (*Lost Boys of Anzac*, 2014)

Very few people in my ancestral family went into military service. Gordon Fink is in my family tree, but out on a distant branch. In 1909, Gordon Fink married Alice Mackie, my mother's mother's father's brother's second-oldest child. Gordon and Alice's marriage was annulled after two years; it was not a divorce. As soon as Australia entered the Great War, Gordon enlisted in the Australian Imperial Force (AIF). He was in the 16th Battalion and was sent to Gallipoli. He died on 2nd May 1915. A tale of heroism? I believe so, but much more complicated than that.

This essay traces the life of Gordon Fink before the war, particularly the demise of his relationship with Alice Mackie. Gordon's father, Theodore Fink, played a pivotal role in the annulment proceedings; he was a powerful man. As the Chairman of Directors at the *Melbourne Herald* he was the man who employed the influential journalist Keith Murdoch (father of Rupert Murdoch).

There are numerous records that relate to Gordon's war service and his death at Gallipoli, just a week after the ANZAC forces landed there. Gordon was part of the Gallipoli saga, part of the ANZAC legend. Newspaper reports gave accounts of Gordon's death, and Australian military sources also provide information. The copious literature on Gallipoli and the Great War offers many perspectives on Gordon's brief, unfortunate stint. A diary by Ellis Silas, another soldier in the 16th Battalion, supplements the literature with the rich, sobering texture of a first-hand account.

Gordon Fink's young days

Gordon's father, Theodore Fink, came to Australia in 1861 from Guernsey in the Channel Islands, as a six-year-old child. Theodore's father, Jewish, was born in Berlin. Theodore was a solicitor, politician and newspaper proprietor who had a prominent career in Victoria. He was a principal of the law firm Fink, Best & Hall.[61] Gordon studied law at Melbourne University, finishing his degree in 1907, but he did not seek admission to the Bar until 1913 in Western Australia (WA).[62]

It seems that Gordon was running away from his family destiny in his father's law firm. He came up to Sydney, and in Sydney he met Alice Mackie, marrying her in 1909 at a Congregational Church.[63] She had been married before, to George Isaacs, but she divorced George in 1907 for

---

[61] Australian Dictionary of Biography, Theodore Fink (1855-1942), https://adb.anu.edu.au/biography/fink-theodore-6171
[62] Death divides comrades, *Weekly Times* (Melbourne), 10 July 1915, p. 31. Retrieved 15 August 2022, from http://nla.gov.au/nla.news-article132700902
[63] Marriage certificate of Gordon Fink and Alice Maud Mackie, married 8 July 1909 at North Sydney, Registry of Births, Deaths and Marriages, New South Wales, 9086/1909.

desertion.[64] She had a daughter, Minnie.[65] After eighteen months of marriage, Gordon and Alice went to Melbourne, presumably to meet Gordon's parents.

What happened in Melbourne was a travesty. A court case for annulment of the marriage was launched on the grounds of Alice's bigamy. She was alleged to still be married to George Isaacs. She was alleged to have told Gordon that George had died. Alice did not appear; she was back in Sydney.[66] The lie is revealed at State Records, Sydney, where the package of divorce papers includes a subpoena from Fink, Best & Hall, seeking custody of the papers.[67]

The stratagem by Gordon's father worked; the marriage was broken up. Subsequently, Gordon joined the Victorian Field Artillery and was a lieutenant, but then he went overseas and joined the Malay States Rifles. He returned to Australia in 1913, but to WA. He was farming with Carl Pirani, a solicitor friend from Melbourne, and was also doing some work as a solicitor.[68]

Years later, Alice married Joseph Beirman, and they remained together for life. (See "Alice and Alice – two cousins", *All the Rivers Come Together*, 2022, pp. 120-131.)

---

[64] Marriage certificate of George Isaacs and Alice Maud Mackie, married 11 April 1902 at Glebe, Registry of Births, Deaths and Marriages, New South Wales, 3912/1902; Divorce Papers, Alice Maud Isaacs and George Isaacs, divorced 14 November 1907, New South Wales State Archives & Records, NRS-13495-28-[13/12657]-6217.

[65] Birth certificate for Minnie Elizabeth Isaacs, born 29 May 1902, Registry of Births, Deaths and Marriages, New South Wales, 18637/1902.

[66] Other divorce cases: Fink v. Isaacs (otherwise Fink), *The Age*, 9 May 1912, p. 11. Retrieved August 15, 2022, from http://nla.gov.au/nla.news-article197366556

[67] See footnote 4.

[68] Death divides comrades, *Weekly Times*, 10 July 1915; Service record of Gordon Fink, Private, 16th Battalion, Australian Imperial Force, National Archives of Australia, B2455, FINK G.

Gordon enlists

Gordon enlisted in September 1914 at Blackboy Hill (WA) with two friends: Pirani, and Harry Leake, a local farmer. They were in the 16th Battalion of the AIF.[69] Despite his former officer rank, Gordon enlisted as a private. Did he have contact with his parents? Not known. With Alice? Not known.

Another recruit to the 16th Battalion was Ellis Silas, who was an artist and who kept a diary.[70] On 18th November 1914, the battalion embarked on the *Dimboola* for Melbourne. They trained at Broadmeadows camp. On 22nd December they sailed on the *Ceramic* for Egypt, and trained at Heliopolis, near Cairo.[71]

The forces that landed at Gallipoli were insufficient, given the strength of the Turkish forces, and the terrain: "It is a military axiom not to advance uphill against the enemy" (*The Art of War*).[72] The plans were fuelled by optimism and British imperial bravado.[73] The historian Hugh Thomas says that Europe had become ardently nationalist in the nineteenth century, that patriotism arose as unquestioning faith in one's country, and "the tide of nationalism was

---

[69] Death divides comrades, *Weekly Times*, 10 July 1915.
[70] Ellis Silas, Biography, Anzac Portal,
https://anzacportal.dva.gov.au/biographies/ellis-luciano-silas
Retrieved 15 August 2022.
[71] Gallipoli diary and sketches by Signaller Ellis Silas,
https://anzacportal.dva.gov.au/wars-and-missions/ww1/where-australians-served/gallipoli/landing-anzac-cove/ellis-silas-diary-extracts
[72] Joan Beaumont, *Broken Nation: Australians in the Great War*, Allen & Unwin, Sydney, 2014, pp. 79-80; *The Art of War*, Sun Tzu, ~500BC, Introduction by Nigel Cawthorne, Arcturus Publishing, London, 2019, chapter 7, v. 33.
[73] Les Carlyon, *Gallipoli*, Macmillan, Sydney, 2001, p.87; Beaumont, 2014, quote from Tim Travers, pp. 66-67.

accompanied by a general romantic disposition to believe that war was glorious".[74]

In 1907, at the British Musketry School in Kent, trials with a machine gun showed that, at 600 yards (550 metres), two Maxim machine guns could wipe out a battalion (roughly 1,000 men) advancing in the open in one minute if the troops did not go to ground.[75] This was an argument of mathematical certainty, an argument that made the gallantry of soldiers irrelevant. The trial was vehemently rejected by the British officers, steeped in centuries of tradition. The planners of Gallipoli simply continued this blithe faith in established ways. They did not see that war had become industrial.

Gallipoli

The attack on Gallipoli began on 25th April 1915. The first troops landed on the beach at 4:30 am. Did they land at the wrong spot? It is generally believed that they did. Regardless, they were fired upon by Turkish troops; but they were ordered to push on at all costs. Losses for the day were heavy, and the troops were not victorious; their positions were precarious. The soldiers were inexperienced, bewildered by the landscape, and shocked by the death and injuries they witnessed.[76]

The 16th Battalion went ashore around 6:00pm, under Colonel John Monash.[77] They were sent immediately to Pope's Hill, where they spent the night digging in. Details of action over the next week in the Battalion diary are

---

[74] Hugh Thomas, *An Unfinished History of the World*, 3rd edition, Macmillan, Sydney, 1995, p. 644.
[75] Les Carlyon, *Gallipoli*, McMillian, Sydney, 2001, p. 198.
[76] Beaumont, 2014, pp. 74-85; Carlyon, 2001, p. 184.
[77] Bringing up ammunition, *Weekly Times* (Melbourne), 17 July 1915, p. 8. Retrieved August 15, 2022, from http://nla.gov.au/nla.news-article132701591

rudimentary.[78] Silas's diary says the 16th held Pope's Hill under constant heavy fire.[79]

On the evening of 2nd May, the 16th Battalion was ordered to take a ridge held by the enemy: Bloody Angle, and hold it until dawn. Fink and Leake were acting as observers to Major W.O. Mansbridge, the company commander.[80] Mansbridge later said, "The men advanced singing 'Tipperary' and telling the Turks in very forcible language what they would do when they got to the top".[81]

Silas said: "Along the ridges and down in the gullies our shells were bursting in clusters. Rifle fire could not be heard through the din".[82] He suffered from shell-shock.[83]

Later in the night the troops were running short of ammunition. "Young Fink" volunteered to carry more ammunition up the ridge in the face of machine-gun fire.[84]

---

[78] AWM423/33/6, April-July 1915, Australian Imperial Force war diaries, 1914-1918 War, 16th Infantry Battalion, Australian War Memorial, https://www.awm.gov.au/collection/C1356592 Retrieved 8 August 2022.
[79] Gallipoli diary and sketches by Signaller Ellis Silas.
[80] Letter of 29 October 1915 from Theodore Fink to Captain J. McLean, Base Records, Victoria Barracks, Melbourne re fate of his son, Gordon Fink, Service record of Gordon Fink, Private, 16th Battalion, Australian Imperial Force, National Archives of Australia, B2455, FINK G.
[81] Major Mansbridge mentions Sgt Carr when describing fight for Pope's Hill, *Kalgoorlie Miner*, WA, 23 October 1915, p. 5, related at Lives of the First World War, https://livesofthefirstworldwar.iwm.org.uk/story/58401 Retrieved 12 August 2022.
[82] 16th Infantry Battalion war diary.
[83] Ellis Silas, Biography, Anzac Portal.
[84] Bringing up ammunition, *Weekly Times* (Melbourne), 17 July 1915. Note, Fink is thirty years old, not an adolescent.

Missing

All the wounded were got in before dawn, and Fink was not among them.[85] Fink was one of a large number of men reported missing, possibly captured.[86] In his War Record, Fink is not listed as missing until 17th May, and it was not until 15th November that he was finally recorded as "Killed In Action".[87] The circumstances were still being investigated on 26th October, largely at the behest of Theodore Fink.[88]

A letter from Theodore Fink to Base Records in Melbourne dated 19th October stated that he had been informed by Brigadier-General Monash's wife in a letter from her husband on 12th May that his opinion was that Gordon Fink had certainly been killed in action.[89] Theodore says that on 1st July he received a letter from Major Mansbridge giving details of Gordon's death. Lieutenant-Colonel Pope wrote to say Gordon had died. Harry Leake wrote to Theodore on 30th July to state that Gordon had died (Leake was wounded in the same battle and was invalided to Egypt).

The authorities in Egypt seem to have known sometime between mid-June and 25th June that Gordon's

---

[85] Major Mansbridge, *Weekly Times*, 17 July 1915.
[86] Soldier possibly captured, *The Herald* (Melbourne), 17 June 1915, p. 12. Retrieved 15 August 2022, from http://nla.gov.au/nla.news-article242368701
[87] Gordon Fink, Service record.
[88] Gordon Fink, Service record: letter sent from Base Records to Theodore Fink in response to a letter from him, informing Fink of enquiries being made in Egypt, but confirming Gordon has been reported as "killed in action" on 2nd May.
[89] Gordon Fink, Service record, letter from Theodore Fink to Base Records.

body had been recognised and his pay book recovered.[90] Also, Theodore says the last letter he wrote to his son was returned to him in mid-October from the Dead Letter Office with the endorsement "Killed".

There is another strand to this account of the determination of Gordon's death. In his letter dated 19th October (referred to above), Gordon's father stated that he made approaches to authorities in London in mid-June, after he had received an official telegram to say his son had been killed. He asked them to investigate further. The Red Cross had set up a branch to carry out investigations into the fate of missing soldiers, and they sent interviewers out to the various arenas of battle. Since the injured from Gallipoli were sent to Egypt, there were interviewers at the hospitals in Alexandria.

A report about Private Gordon Fink from the 16th Battalion is contained in the "Australian Red Cross Wounded and Missing" files.[91] It is dated 26th June 1915. The transcript reads: "Was shot through the head during a bayonet charge on a Sunday, either 2nd or 9th May [1915]. Had been acting as trench observer to Major Maxbridge [Mansbridge] of 'A' Company. Body was found some days afterwards and identified by under signed who was in camp with him in Melbourne. Father is stated to be interested in the 'Melbourne Herald'."

The informant was Private Tom Bolton, who was then at the 17th General Hospital in Alexandria. A footnote to the report says the enquiry was initiated in London. Several questions are raised by this report. According to Major Mansbridge's account, Gordon was carrying ammunition up

[90] Gordon Fink, Stories from the Memorial Board, A Supreme Court of Victoria and Legal Profession First World War Commemoration. Pdf retrieved 28 March 2016.
[91] Australian War Memorial archives, https://www.awm.gov.au/collection/R1486763

the ridge, which does not suggest a bayonet attack. More fundamentally, Bolton's war record says he was wounded on 30th April. He sustained a bayonet wound to his right leg and he was taken out to the hospital in Egypt. The Red Cross report says that Bolton identified Gordon's body, but Bolton was not at Gallipoli at the time. Bolton did not return to his unit until 14th July.[92]

No doubt everyone was wanting certainty in this situation. Perhaps Tom Bolton had heard a story about Gordon Fink from someone else, so was passing it on in order to be of help. Bolton is correct about other particulars – the commander of the company was Major Mansbridge, and Gordon had been a trench observer for him, and Gordon's father was "interested in the 'Melbourne Herald'".

Theodore's many letters suggest he was distraught. He urges reform of the communications system so that relatives of soldiers receive "more rapid communication" about missing soldiers. However, the 16th Battalion had "a casualty list of 800 out of its original strength of 1,023 of all ranks" in two months.[93] With the troops under constant heavy fire, it was often days or weeks before dead men could be retrieved, identified and buried.[94] It must have been chaotic as well as horrifying.

---

[92] Service record of Tom Bolton, Private, 16th Battalion, Australian Imperial Force, National Archives of Australia, B2455, BOLTON T.

[93] Life laid down for men in firing line at dawn, *The Herald* (Melbourne), 10 July 1915, p. 1. (The reference to dawn is misplaced.)

[94] Gallipoli diary and sketches by Signaller Ellis Silas. An expedition in January 1919 found numerous relics of the 16th Battalion's battles – human bones, tattered pieces of uniform, the Rising Sun badge. Relics of the 16th Battalion at the Bloody Angle, Gallipoli, 1919: https://www.awm.gov.au/articles/blog/relics-of-the-16th-battalion-at-the-bloody-angle-gallipoli-1919

Aftermath

Mansbridge gave a tribute to Gordon and his comrades in July 1915: "The charge of this battalion, in which young Fink took part, was one of the most glorious and most gallant of the many fine feats of arms which stand to the credit of the Australian soldiers."[95]

But it is also true, as *The Art of War* says, that "soldiers when in desperate straits lose the sense of fear. If there is no help for it, they will fight hard".[96]

However, Gordon's motivations for enlisting do not seem to be merely patriotism. The circumstances suggest that, with his marriage to Alice destroyed by his father, he felt he had nothing to live for. And, perhaps after the debacle of the annulment, Gordon needed to show himself to be brave.

The battalion served at Gallipoli until the evacuation in December.[97]

Gordon's sister, Margery, donated £25 for the endowment of a cot in the Base Hospital, Melbourne, to be called "The Gordon Fink Cot".[98]

Gordon's father was sent Gordon's 1914/1915 Star, Victory Medal and British War Medal in the period 1920-1922.[99]

---

[95] W.A. Hero, *Daily News* (Perth), 12 July 1915, p. 6. Retrieved 12 August 2022, from http://nla.gov.au/nla.news-article80997518.

[96] *The Art of War*, Chapter 11, v. 24.

[97] Description of 16th Battalion, Australian War Memorial, https://www.awm.gov.au/collection/U51456 Retrieved 14 August 2022; Frank Welsh, *Great Southern Land*, Penguin, London, 2004, p. 368.

[98] Endowment of cot, *Argus* (Melbourne), 8 May 1916, p. 8. Retrieved 16 August 2022, from http://nla.gov.au/nla.news-article2110560

[99] Gordon Fink, Service record.

A memorial for Gordon at Lone Pine Cemetery was ordered 19th February 1926.[100]

Alice Fink (Mackie) got married again on 25th August 1916.[101] It is notable that Alice had kept the name Fink; she could have reverted to Isaacs or Mackie. It is also notable that Gordon's marriage to Alice is not mentioned in any of the public accounts of Gordon's life.

Alice did not forget Gordon Fink and his death in war. On 3 December 1943 she inserted a notice in a newspaper column's Roll of Honour for her nephew, Flight-Sergeant N.M. Davis. He was her older sister's son.

References

Primary sources

Argus (Melbourne).

Australian Dictionary of Biography, https://adb.anu.edu.au/

Australian Imperial Force war diaries, 1914-1918 War, 16th Infantry Battalion, Australian War Memorial, https://www.awm.gov.au/collection/C1356592

Australian War Memorial, https://www.awm.gov.au/

Description of 16th Battalion, Australian War Memorial, https://www.awm.gov.au/collection/U51456

Ellis Silas, Biography, Anzac Portal, https://anzacportal.dva.gov.au/biographies/ellis-luciano-silas

Gallipoli diary and sketches by Signaller Ellis Silas, Anzac Portal, https://anzacportal.dva.gov.au/

---

[100] Gordon Fink, Service record; Memorial for Private Gordon Fink, Lone Pine, Commonwealth War Graves Commission.
[101] Marriage certificate of David Thomas McLoughlin and Alice Fink, married at Randwick on 25 August 1916, Registry of Births, Deaths and Marriages, New South Wales, 10332/1916.

Lives of the First World War,
https://livesofthefirstworldwar.iwm.org.uk/

New South Wales State Archives & Records.

Registry of Births, Deaths and Marriages, New South Wales.

Relics of the 16th Battalion at the Bloody Angle, Gallipoli, 1919:
https://www.awm.gov.au/articles/blog/relics-of-the-16th-battalion-at-the-bloody-angle-gallipoli-1919

Service record of Gordon Fink, Private, 16th Battalion, Australian Imperial Force, National Archives of Australia, B2455, FINK G.

Stories from the Memorial Board, A Supreme Court of Victoria and Legal Profession First World War Commemoration.

The Age (Melbourne).

The Herald (Melbourne).

Weekly Times (Melbourne).

Secondary sources

Beaumont, Joan, *Broken Nation: Australians in the Great War*, Allen & Unwin, Sydney, 2014.

Carlyon, Les, *Gallipoli*, Macmillan, Sydney, 2001.

Sun Tzu, *The Art of War*, Introduction by Nigel Cawthorne, Arcturus Publishing, London, 2019.

Thomas, Hugh, *An Unfinished History of the World*, 3rd edition, Macmillan, Sydney, 1995.

Welsh, Frank, *Great Southern Land*, Penguin, London, 2004.

Image 4.1 (from top left) Gordon Fink; newspaper headline from *The Daily News*, Perth, 11 July 1915; Harry Leake and Gordon Fink, in *The Weekly Times* (Melbourne), 10 July 1915.

Image 4.2: Lone Pine memorial, Gordon Fink, died 2 May 1915. (Commonwealth War Graves)

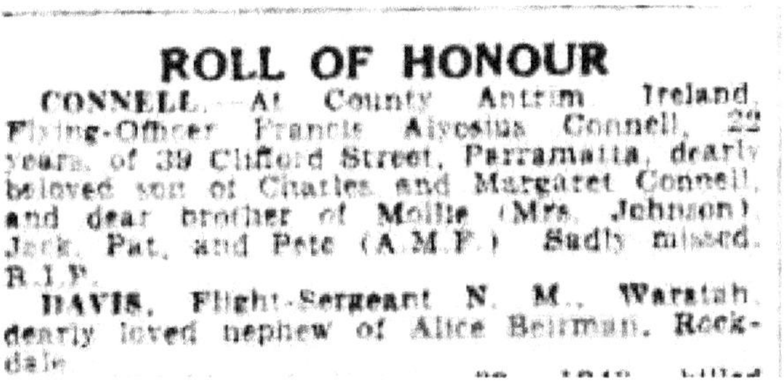

ROLL OF HONOUR

CONNELL.—At County Antrim Ireland, Flying-Officer Francis Aloysius Connell, 22 years, of 39 Clifford Street, Parramatta, dearly beloved son of Charles and Margaret Connell, and dear brother of Mollie (Mrs. Johnson) Jack, Pat, and Pete (A.M.F.) Sadly missed. R.I.P.

DAVIS. Flight-Sergeant N. M., Waratah, dearly loved nephew of Alice Beirman, Rockdale.

Image 4.3: Alice's notice in the Roll of Honour for her sister's son, *Sydney Morning Herald*, 3 December 1943.

5 Love in Wartime

I was filling in gaps in my family tree. When I started doing family history, I was looking backwards. Once I had found a couple in one generation, I looked backwards to find their parents. But now I have a very large family tree, and I find myself looking forwards again. A particular couple might have several children, and I begin to wonder about the children, and what happened to them.

Edwin and Ellen Eaglestone are great grandparents of mine, on my father's side. Edwin was a stonemason. He was born in England in 1858, but he came to Australia with his parents when he was one. Edwin and Ellen lived in a stone house at Balmain. They had three girls who grew up and married. One of them was my grandmother, Elizabeth Hannah Eaglestone, who married William Thomas Martin, my grandfather. But what happened to her two sisters, Sarah Ellen and Blanche Ellen?

Sarah married Herbert Lappan, who was a saddler, in Sydney in 1902. They had four children, and then she died, a while after the birth of the last child. She was still very young, only twenty-five. That was a sad story. Herbert married again: Kathleen Goodwin, for whom this was her first marriage, at twenty-nine, but they had no children, and she died but three years later.

Blanche, the youngest child of Edwin and Ellen Eaglestone, married young; she was only seventeen. She married another Herbert: Herbert Augustus Royall, who was initially an electrician, but who became a pay clerk for a large company. They had eight children: four boys and four girls, but two of the boys died young. And the marriage was not a happy one; it split up. Herbert had custody of the children, and he lived for a time with his parents, but then he married again, and had three more children with his second wife.

All of Herbert and Blanche Royall's children got married. It was the marriage of Ellen Mary Royall that interested me. She was in the middle; she had one older sister and two younger sisters. The entry in Births Deaths and Marriages said Ellen's husband's name was "Siegfried Emil Heinrich Freiherr von Einsiedel / Hottelmann", and the date was 1939. What's more, there were five entries for the same record, Registration No. 13886/1939. The entries had variations of the husband's surname. The marriage took place in Rockdale, Sydney.

This was enough to invite further investigation. It appeared that Siegfried was German, and being in Sydney at that time (only a couple of months before the Second World War started), and marrying into a family whose history was all British and a touch of Irish, was intriguing. Ellen's name came from her grandmother, Ellen Elizabeth Lewis. Both of Ellen Lewis's parents had been convicts, one English, one Irish. Ellen Lewis was the one that married the stonemason.

I obtained the marriage certificate for Siegfried and Ellen. It said he was born in Germany, at Holzminden in Saxony. It said he was a salesman, and she was a dressmaker. Siegfried's father had been an engineer (both his parents were deceased). It also said his father's name was Hottelmann and his mother's name was von Einsiedel. One has to ask, why is his mother's name seeming to compete with his father's name?

Unusually, the marriage record has a long, handwritten note next to it, dated 28 January 1948, after the end of the war. Originally the husband's name was Siegfried Emil Hottelmann, but the note seeks to change the name from Hottelmann to von Einsiedel, but to still acknowledge "Hottelmann" as being the name by which he is known. The handwritten note says his full name was "Siegfried Emil Freiherr von Einsiedel known as Hottelmann". I didn't know it at the time, but the name "Freiherr" signifies that the person is a German baron.

But was he a salesman? And was he really a baron? And how did he and Ellen meet?

What I discovered was that he was a sailor, and he deserted ship in Adelaide in September 1938. He had a passport issued at Hamburg in 1935, and he left Germany permanently in 1936. He went to America on the ship *Hagen*, and apparently stayed in America for two years. He spoke English well, and even acquired an American twang. He was in San Francisco in late July 1938, where he joined the *M.S. Tisnaren*, a Swedish merchant ship carrying cargo around the world. It had just come from Vancouver with a load of timber for Australia. It arrived in Sydney on 25 August, but was only there for a day. It sailed to Melbourne and stayed for several days while timber was unloaded.

The *Tisnaren* went to Adelaide and was there for six days, unloading, then it left, bound for Queensland to pick up 8,700 tons of sugar to transport to London. When the ship left Adelaide, Siegfried was not on it: he had deserted. He was reported to the authorities, because he was an "alien" under Australian law.

Later, I learned that when he was in Melbourne, he had visited the Immigration Department and requested permission to stay in Australia permanently. In the interim, he worked on a coastal ship, returning to Adelaide between trips until March 1939, when he received the approval for permanent residency.

Siegfried got more work on a coastal ship, but was paid off when the ship was in Sydney and it needed to stay for repairs. It was then that he became, briefly, a salesman. He later admitted that he did not make a success of it. And during this period, he met Ellen Royall and after a lightning romance, he married her. But how did they meet?

My best guess was: at the circus. Siegfried's past was full of adventure. He had visited Australia previously, from 1928 to 1930. During this time, he had stowed away to New Zealand and joined Wirth's Circus while it toured around the two islands. He was an attendant for the elephants. No experience, and apparently none required, just a conviction that he could do it. Perhaps it was no coincidence that the Wirth brothers were German.

So, Siegfried was in Sydney in April 1939, and he secured lodgings at Kings Cross. And he discovered that Wirth's Circus had come to town, and it was just down the road in William Street. Wouldn't he visit it, I thought, to reignite the memories of his youthful adventures? And Ellen Royall worked in the city, at the Dymock's building in George Street, making dresses. She would have heard that the circus was coming to town. Wouldn't she go? It was billed as the "Greatest Show on Earth"!

Later, as I got further into my research, I discovered that my surmise was wrong, and they did not meet at the circus. They met at the Tivoli in George Street. This is just as good a story! The Tivoli was the place to go at night in Sydney in the 1930s. My mother told me she used to go there as a young woman, to dances and dinners, which happened most days of the week. It was the place to meet new people.

Within six weeks, Siegfried and Ellen had tied the knot (1st July 1939), in a simple ceremony at the registry office at Rockdale, near where she lived in a boarding house, in the presence of her sisters and friends. Her father refused to have anything to do with Siegfried; he was a German! But Ellen and Siegfried were in love. And Siegfried had not said that he was a baron. He was simply Siegfried Hottelmann, currently a salesman, and usually, a sailor. And he had the status of being a permanent resident of Australia. He was not about to be thrown out.

It is no surprise, however, that after the war started, Siegfried was put into a detention camp. He was a German, recently arrived, so he was inherently suspicious. There were all sorts of stories about him; apparently that was common at the time. It was said that he travelled back and forth to Germany, that he was a spy. It was said he had a radio, and used it when he was out at sea to communicate back to the Nazis. It was said he was a leader of the Nazis in Hamburg. He supposedly said that the English had started the war.

He was sent to the internment camp set up for Germans at Tatura in Victoria. By now, Ellen had a baby, and she was finding it difficult to live alone. But she could not live with her parents, because of her father's attitude towards Germans. So, she asked to be interned along with Siegfried. In 1942, the authorities agreed, and she and the baby went to join him.

It was here, among other Germans, that she learned that her husband was a Baron, because some of the other German interns knew this. He had to tell her that he was heir to the title Baron von Einsiedel, and heir to the lands, but he had fled from a grandfather who was "too severe to live with".

They spent the war in the camp, for the time being just an ordinary family. After the war ended they were released, and they forged a life in the outer suburbs of Sydney. There were three children by then. Siegfried went back to being a sailor on merchant ships.

All this a family can conceal: a man who left an aristocratic family in Europe and emigrated to Australia, who got out of Hitler's Germany and was then locked up for the duration of the war, an adventurer who travelled the world as a youth and even joined the circus to look after the elephants. And Ellen, the girl who fell in love with a nobleman and stood by him through all his trials.

Siegfried may have gone on a trip back to Germany in 1972, but if so, it was a brief trip, and he returned to Ellen in Sydney. He did not repeat the trip. He died in 1980, still just a sailor, and with no signs of his previous status.

*   *   *   *   *

The above story is a snapshot from the book, *The Sailor, the Baron and the Dressmaker* (2024).

Image 5.1: Swedish merchant ship, *Tisnaren* (from website Warsailors.com)

Image 5.2: Siegfried Hottelmann and Ellen Royall (National Archives of Australia)

6 Betsy and the Emperor

Part 1: My connection to Betsy Balcombe

My family is, in worldly terms, undistinguished. There are no social or political leaders, no wealthy people, nor even any significantly infamous scoundrels. I have discovered, over many years, thousands of individuals who are part of my family tree, so it is ostensibly a good-sized sample of the population. They are, for the most part, workers: tradesmen, dressmakers, servants, namely, people who work to earn a living.

Accordingly, I was much surprised to come across a story involving a friendship between Napoleon, the would-be emperor of all of Europe, and a young girl, Betsy Balcombe, a girl with whom I have a family connection. Emperors, even defeated ones, move in rarified atmospheres, so I wondered what my connection could be with someone who was called a friend of Napoleon's. It was a long thread: it takes thirteen steps in the family tree to get from me to Betsy, but it is nevertheless real.

I had been working on my family's history for a few years, long enough to discover the truth behind some of my mother's stories. I had got back to my great great grandparents' generation and discovered there was a convict in the family. My mother had said, adamantly and like a mantra, "There are no convicts in our family", meaning her side of the family. It seemed to be a question of defending one's social standing.

However, in fact, her great grandfather had been a convict. William Archer, born in 1813 in Hertfordshire,

England, was a groom. His crime was to steal 28 pairs of "high shoes", and he was caught. He was sentenced to be transported to the colony of New South Wales for seven years. He had probably worked at a hotel, looking after the horses. An opportunity had come along to make a few pounds, but he hadn't been able to pull it off. He was shipped out on the *Waterloo,* arriving in Sydney in February 1838.

However, Willliam was not defeated. He worked out his sentence on a farm in the Hunter valley, married Ellen Welch, who had come to Australia from Scotland as an assisted migrant: young, single, female. They had eight children together. Willliam and Ellen went back to England in the late 1860s for a few years, working an orchard in Kent, but then they returned to Australia.

William went on to establish a hotel at Pyrmont (Sydney) in the 1880s and he was the publican up until his death. Note, his father had been a labourer in Hertfordshire, but later in life he had become a brewer. William and his wife sought to improve their social standing, despite the difficulty he had in this endeavour, having been a convict. William purchased a large grave site at Waverley Cemetery where William, Ellen, and eighteen other relatives are interred. It has an obelisk at the centre which is about three metres high.

And from here there is a connection to Betsy. The fifth of William and Ellen's children was Hellen Elizabeth Archer, born in 1854 in the Hunter valley. She had gone to England with her parents, but she met a young man in London: Arthur Edwin Gibson, a carpenter. While her parents went back to Australia, Hellen stayed in London and married Arthur. It was 1880 before they came back to Australia. She and Arthur brought their one child with them, and Hellen was heavily pregnant with their second child.

The second child was born in February 1881, soon after their arrival in Sydney, and she was named Edith

Amelia Maud Gibson. They had six more children, but it is Edith who is of interest here. She married Harry Edward Longmore Gengoult Smith (1883-1936), a tram conductor, who was also born in Sydney.

Edith and Harry had two children, called Helen (born 1910) and Harry (born 1916). Helen lived to be one hundred. She worked at Clifford Love's bakery (Uncle Toby's Oats) all her working life and she never married. When she was young she was engaged to a man, Robert Samuel Fulton. When World War 2 was declared, he joined the Royal Australian Engineers and was sent to Lebanon as a Lance Sergeant in the 215 Field Company. He was killed in 1941 and is buried in the War Cemetery in Lebanon. After this experience, Helen did not marry. She died in 2010 and is one of the family members who is buried in the William Archer grave at Waverley.

Not much is known about Harry. He married Eva Prideaux in 1939 and they had three children. He survived his wife and lived to be eighty-one. He died in Katoomba.

Helen and Harry's father's parents, Edward Longmore Gengoult Smith and Minnie Goodacre, also lived in Sydney. Harry (born 1883) had been born a year after they married. After twenty years of marriage they were divorced, on the grounds of Edward's cruelty and adultery. She married again soon afterwards, and he also remarried.

Edward's long name seemed to indicate social standing, so I followed him. He had been born in Melbourne, and his father was Dr Louis Lawrence Smith. Edward's mother was Sarah Ann Taylor. Edward was the third of ten children. After Louis's wife died, he married again, to Marion Jane Higgins, and one of their four children, (Sir) Harold Gengoult Smith, became the Lord Mayor of Melbourne.

At this point we are getting closer to my connection with young Betsy, and the connection is through the two marriages of Doctor Louis. Edward (from the first marriage) was the step-brother of Sir Harold (who was from the second marriage).

Dr Louis Lawrence Smith (1830-1910) was an interesting man. He was a medical practitioner and politician. He was born in London, and he studied medicine in London and Paris. He was apprenticed for five years to the surgeon Sir Thomas Longmore; thus we know where the name Longmore came from.

Dr Smith came to Australia in 1852 as a ship's surgeon and stayed. He established a medical practice in Melbourne, which thrived. He adopted innovative approaches, and issued an annual medical almanac. Despite opposition from some medical professionals, he became a prominent figure and earned a substantial income from his practice.

Dr Smith entered politics on the strength of his forceful personality, and he had an active political life. He died in 1910. Given Dr Smith's forceful personality and a multitude of children, there are plenty of reasons to explain why Edward might have exited the scene and headed to Sydney, despite having been given both the names of historical significance.

"Longmore" came from the surgeon in London to whom Dr Louis Smith had been apprenticed when young. The name "Gengoult" comes from his mother. His father, Edward Tyrell Smith, had been a theatrical entrepreneur in London, and he married a lady from The Netherlands, Madeleine Nanette Gengoult.

Our interest now is in Edward's step-brother, Sir Harold Gengoult Smith (1890-1983), and the woman he married: Cynthia Mary Emmerton Brookes. The thread leads from them upwards to Betsy. Harold became the Lord Mayor of Melbourne, but prior to that he trained as a medical practitioner in Scotland and he served as a soldier in World War I, followed by service with the Red Cross.

After his return to Australia he was elected to Melbourne City Council, and in 1931 he was elected as Lord Mayor, Melbourne's first bachelor mayor. He was immensely popular, and when he married Cynthia Mary Emmerton Brookes in 1933 at St Paul's Church of England Cathedral, their wedding attracted tens of thousands of onlookers. Cynthia was the daughter of Sir Norman and Mabel Brookes. She was 21 and he was 43.

Harold was knighted in 1934. He was involved in organising the celebrations for Victoria's centenary in 1934. Following this he retired as mayor, but he continued as a councillor for the next thirty years.

Cynthia (1912-1961) also came from a prominent family. Her parents were Norman Everard Brookes (1877-1968) and Mabel Balcombe Emmerton (1890-1975). Norman was knighted in 1939 for public services in Australia, and Mabel was made a Dame in 1955 for charitable and social welfare services. Norman was famous as an Australian tennis player: the first non-British player to win Wimbledon, in 1907 and 1914. He was also the first left-hander to win the title.

Norman was also part of the Davis Cup team that won the title six times. The current Australian Open men's singles trophy is named after him. He was president of the Lawn Tennis Association of Australia for 29 years. In business life he went to work at Australian Paper Mills, where his father was the managing director. Within eight years, Norman was a member of the board.

Norman and Mabel became a leading part of Melbourne's social life. They hosted entertainments at their home. At the end of World War 2 their home was the venue for social events for Australian and American military officers, among whom was Lyndon Baines Johnson. When Johnson visited Australia in 1966 as President of the United States of America, he again visited their home.

Mabel was said to be the undisputed social leader of support for hospitals and charities in Melbourne. She was the only child of Harry Emmerton, a solicitor who had emigrated from England as a child, and Alice Mabel Maude, born Balcombe. Mabel was a grand-daughter of Alexander Balcombe, Betsy's youngest brother.

Harry Emmerton was born on his father's estate in Buckinghamshire and he came to Australia when he was four, in 1849. His ancestors had provided auditors and notaries for the royal courts of King Henry VIII and Queen Elizabeth I, so it was appropriate that he should study law. He spent his entire working life as a solicitor with the firm J. M. Smith and Emmerton in Melbourne. He was a member of the Melbourne Club, a member of numerous boards, and was honorary legal adviser to many charities.

Alice Balcombe, Harry Emmerton's wife, took on the role of hostess, organising many events at their home for charitable and artistic causes. They also played host to prominent people visiting Melbourne. She was patron of several musical and art societies. In later life, she was made an Officer of the British Empire.

Alice's father was Alexander Beatson Balcombe (1811-1877), and Betsy Balcombe was Alexander's older sister. Thus we have a chain of thirteen links from Glenn Martin through to Betsy Balcombe. Alexander was a small boy (and the youngest child) when Napoleon was exiled to St Helena, while Betsy had just turned thirteen. Napoleon lived on the island from October 1815 until his death in May 1821.

Part 2: The Balcombe family and St Helena

Betsy's parents were William Tomset Balcombe and Jane Byng, who had got married in London in 1799 at St Marylebone Parish Church. There were varying versions of William's parenthood. His parents were (probably) Stephen

Balcombe and Mary Vandyke. Stephen was the captain of a frigate and he lost his life at sea in a boating accident. He may have been a privateer, or involved in smuggling. Another story was that he was the son of the landlord of the New Ship Inn at Brighton.

Under the "lost at sea" story, the Prince Regent (later King George IV) had a charity for children whose fathers had been lost at sea, and William was a beneficiary of this charity. It also meant the existence of patronage, and William went to sea at a young age as a "captain's servant", and soon became a midshipman. He also enjoyed the protection and support of Sir Thomas Tyrwitt, who was the private secretary of the Prince Regent.

An associated story was that William was actually the biological son of the Prince Regent, even though the Prince Regent would have been only fifteen at the time. The story floated around as a rumour for years, and preceded him to St Helena. If it were true, this would have been a compelling reason that William received patronage. However, the more likely story is that the death of Stephen Balcombe at sea was caused by the Prince Regent's yacht colliding with his boat. This is the story that is accepted by the descendants of William Balcombe.

Anne Whitehead (*Betsy and the Emperor*, 2015) suggested that Napoleon cultivated a friendship with the Balcombe family by design, because it was known that William was connected with Sir Thomas Tyrwitt, who was in turn connected with British royalty. Napoleon was still hoping to be able to leave the island, and those connections might be helpful to such a purpose.

The patronage and periodic active support of Sir Thomas Tyrwitt is evident at various points of William's career. Willliam grew up and obtained various positions. In 1805 he obtained a position on the island of St Helena with the East India Company, as superintendent of public sales, but he also had interests as a senior partner in the firm Balcombe, Cole and Company, which supplied provisions to vessels calling at the island.

William brought his family with him: his wife, Jane, and two girls. The first child, Jane, was born in 1800; the second, Lucia Elizabeth (who became Betsy), was born in 1802. After arrival on the island there was another daughter, Mary, but she died of measles as an infant. There were subsequently three more children, all born on St Helena: William (1808), Thomas Tyrwitt (1810) and Alexander Beatson (1811). Later, the two girls went back to England to attend boarding school in Nottingham.

Notably, Thomas has 'Tyrwitt' as a middle name. The 'Beatson' in Alexander's name, as well as the 'Alexander', came from Major General Alexander Beatson, who was the governor of St Helena from 1808 to 1813. It indicates that William Balcombe had a congenial relationship with the governor. The convention was that the person whose name had been so honoured was the child's godfather.

At boarding school the children were told the terrible tales of Napoleon's marauding in Europe, including his ill-fated Russian expedition, when hundreds of thousands of troops died, not just in battle, but of starvation and frostbite, and injured horses were left to die in the snow. Betsy heard about Moscow being set on fire by its inhabitants so that there was nothing for him to win. (This may not have been the truth, but the sentiment against Napoleon was strong.)

Added to the horrible stories about the devastation that Napoleon had caused, Betsy had nightmares about the man. She pictured him as a giant ogre with one flaming red eye, protruding teeth with which he would tear prey to pieces, especially little girls who misbehaved, and he had a vast cape which cloaked much of Europe. At thirteen, she retained that childish terror.

St Helena is an island of volcanic rock with an area of around 200 square kilometres, in the middle of the southern Atlantic Ocean. It is 1,800 kilometres from the nearest land in Africa, and over 3,220 kilometres from the Brazilian coast. It is one of the most remote places on Earth. It was uninhabited until it was discovered by Portuguese seafarers in 1502. It was colonised by Britain to use as a waystation for the East India Company in 1658, and the island became a British overseas territory.

The Governor of the territory in 1815 was Mark Wilks, and it was a quiet existence on the island. Mail from London took ten weeks to arrive. Ships called at the island frequently for fresh water and provisions, on their way to the Middle East or returning from there to England, but there was little to disturb everyday life. There were 1,150 civilians, 1,000 soldiers, and 1,400 slaves living on the island. The island needed to be protected, as it was a valuable asset, and there was a war going on with the French.

When St Helena had been colonised, the use of slaves was commonplace. It was described as a "mild" form of slavery, more like serfdom, but slaves could be bought and sold. Slaves were first brought from East Africa or Madagascar, and later from Malaysia and India. St Helena stopped importing slaves in 1792, and in 1807 the slave trade was banned throughout the British Empire. This did not, however, free existing slaves. The first step towards eliminating slavery on the island was made in 1818.

William Balcombe and family lived at 'The Briars', a lovely homestead among the hills about two kilometres from Jamestown (the only town). The cottage was modest, but it had an extensive garden that included briar roses. It also had a separate Pavilion where visitors stayed and where balls were occasionally held. William's interests, separate from the East India Company, included an orchard, a large vegetable garden, and a brewery. The household kept several slaves, who worked in the garden and the house.

The news of Napoleon's coming, which was accompanied by a change to direct British government rule rather than being under the East India Company's jurisdiction, was a colossal upheaval for the island. Willliam Balcombe, courtesy of his connection with Sir Thomas Tyrwitt, received a letter on the same ship that brought news to the island that the defeated emperor, Napoleon Bonaparte, was coming, and he was to be a prisoner of state on the island.

The letter informed him that he was to be appointed Naval Agent, which meant he would be responsible for supplying all the provisions needed by Napoleon and his entourage. This private information was soon confirmed by Admiral Sir George Cockburn, who brought the prisoner Napoleon to the island following his capture.

The British victors had decided they would not allow Napoleon to live in England. Instead, they would send him somewhere remote, from where he was less likely to escape. This was understandable, given that when Napoleon had been defeated before, the Bourbon King had been restored in France, and Napoleon was exiled to the tiny island of Elba off the coast of Italy. But within ten months he had escaped and built another army.

Wellington had beaten Napoleon at the Battle of Waterloo in June 1815. This was the final battle. Napoleon's resurgence had only lasted One Hundred Days. At the age of forty-six, Napoleon's days of dominating Europe were over. His first thought was to escape to the United States, but when he arrived at the port of Rochefort in southern France, the British were waiting. He surrendered on the ship *HMS Bellerophon*. At this stage, Napoleon thought he would be allowed to live in England.

However, the British made the decision to send Napoleon to St Helena. Wellington had in fact stayed on the island at 'The Briars' in earlier years, and he thought it would be a suitable prison: not a gaol with bars, but still a place from which there were no means of escape.

Napoleon was sent on the ship *Northumberland*. The sloop-of-war, *Icarus*, which carried the momentous news, arrived only four days before the prisoner himself.

Part 3: The friendship between Napoleon and Betsy

When Napoleon finally disembarked from the ship at Jamestown, the entire population turned out to see him. They had only recently found out that he had escaped from the island of Elba to rise again, so it was a further shock to find that he was now a prisoner of the British.

The first night, Napoleon stayed at a lodging house in the town, but the great man made it clear that he would not tolerate being constantly ogled. He refused to accept that even now he was anything less than the Emperor Napoleon: "Je ne suis pas le Général Bonaparte, je suis L'Empereur Napoléon." (I am not General Bonaparte, I am the Emperor Napoleon.) This sentiment remained to the end of his life.

The idea was for him to be lodged at Longwood, high up in the hills in the interior of the island, but on inspection, the house was found to be in need of significant repairs and renovations. Admiral Cockburn agreed that Napoleon could visit 'The Briars', since it had already been mentioned as a possibility, and the Governor of the island was not prepared to give up his own residence, 'Plantation House'.

They rode to the house on horseback. The family was sitting out on the lawn in the afternoon sun, and Betsy's first sight of Napoleon was impressive: he on a black charger with crimson saddle cloth and gold trimmings, and wearing the outfit for which he was famous: green felt jacket, white breeches and tricorne hat. He conversed with William and Jane Balcombe, but as his English was poor, and their French was not much better, Betsy, as the most well-versed in French, came into the conversation.

She took the opportunity to scrutinise him. She thought that his smile was fascinating, and his manner was kind, far from the ogre she had pictured. She thought his appearance was remarkable, and that his smile, and the expression of his eye, were such that they could not be conveyed in a painting.

Dame Mabel Brookes, in her book (1961), says this meeting was the moment when Napoleon stepped down from world domination into the anti-climax of a garden and an English family. "The charger that had brought him to the gate of The Briars was the final expression of the pageantry of the past."

Napoleon questioned Betsy on geography. What is the capital of France? Paris. What is the capital of Italy? Rome. And of Russia? She replied, "Petersburg now; formerly, Moscow."

At this, he stared at her intensely: "Qui l'a brulé?" (Who burned it?) She was seized by panic and was only able to say, "I do not know, sir." Whereupon he exclaimed, "Oui, oui, vous savez très bien, c'est moi qui l'a brulé!" (Yes, yes, you know very well, it was me that burned it!)

In her innocence, Betsy found a little courage, and a response: "I believe, sir, the Russians burned it to get rid of the French."

But Napoleon liked The Briars, and wanted to stay. Arrangements were made for him immediately. The Pavilion was reorganised and prepared, and he slept there that night. In the evening, he came into the house, and asked Betsy if she was familiar with music. He added, "You are too young to play yourself." Betsy told him she could both sing and play, and she sang him a Scottish song, "Ye banks and braes".

Napoleon admired her singing and playing. They spoke comfortably in French. This was the beginning of their friendship. He spent about three months at The Briars, until Longwood was ready to be occupied. He had an entourage, and a large marquee had been erected for them. There were about twenty people, officers and other staff. They included his personal secretary, Count de Las Cases, the generals Gourgaud, Betrand and de Montholon, plus servants and various wives and children.

A book (*Napoleon: The Last Phase*) by the Earl of Rosebery, published in 1900, said, "When the Balcombe girls met Napoleon they were able to converse with him in French, Betsy was the prettier and more outgoing of the two and represented a type of girl new to the Emperor. She was considered to be a high-spirited 'hoyden', a bold, bordering-on-rude young tomboy, who said and did whatever occurred on the spur of the moment."

Betsy later wrote of Napoleon, "He seemed to enter into every sort of mirth or fun with the glee of a child". She wrote, "I have often tried his patience severely, (but) I never knew him lose his temper or fall back on his rank or age".

The situation seemed to give Napoleon the chance to let go of the weight of his former worldly role and his ambitions. He could relax without any of the expectations of court or the rigorous necessities of military command. Yet he lived simply, so he was not put out by the circumstances. He did not expect banquets; he ate his meals promptly and left the table. It was as if this was life on another campaign. He had a daily routine, part of which was to dictate his memoirs to Las Cases, who was his secretary, and this was interspersed with, of all things, playing games with the children.

Betsy found his manner "so unaffectedly kind and amiable, that in a few days I felt perfectly at ease in his society, and looked at him more as a companion of my own age than as the mighty warrior at whose name 'the world grew pale'." It was in 1844 (at the age of forty-two) that she finally wrote an account of this period of time (but she had notes she had written years before). It was published in London as "Recollections of the Emperor Napoleon on the Island of St Helena, including the time of his residence at her father's house, 'The Briars'".

Her book recounts many lively episodes at The Briars. Napoleon's affection for her seems genuine, and she seems also to have served a need he had at that time: all his great plans were ruined, and he was separated from his family (his wife, Marie Louise, Archduchess of Austria, and a child, Napoleon Francis Joseph Charles, known from birth as the King of Rome). Likewise, Betsy seems to have had a genuine affection for Napoleon. It was a switch from her original terror of him, and it is clear that she felt safe with him.

There was one episode where Napoleon had teased her by saying she should marry the son of Las Cases. The boy was only a year older than Betsy. Napoleon even urged him to kiss her hand, and he did. Betsy was outraged, and boxed the boys' ears. But she was also determined to punish Napoleon himself.

One day soon after, a small party was making its way down a steep, narrow rocky path to play a game of whist. The party consisted of Napoleon at the front, then Las Cases, his son, and Jane (Betsy's older sister). Betsy was at the back. She waited until she was about ten metres behind, then ran full tilt towards them all, pushing her sister hard in the back. She in turn catapulted into Las Cases' son, Las Cases, and the emperor, who stumbled and had difficulty in preserving his footing.

Betsy said, "I was in ecstasies at the confusion I had created, and exulted in the revenge I had taken for the kiss." She describes Las Cases as being thunderstruck at the insult offered to the emperor, and he became furious. He seized her by the shoulders and shook her. Then it was her turn to be enraged, and she burst into tears of passion. She turned to Napoleon and cried out, "Oh, sir, he has hurt me!"

"Never mind," replied the emperor, "I will hold him while you punish him." And she boxed his ears until he begged for mercy. But then Napoleon told him to run, and if he could not run faster than her, he deserved to be beaten again. And he clapped his hands and laughed in glee. She said Las Cases did not like her after that.

On another occasion, Napoleon and Betsy had been discussing swords, and (Betsy wrote) Napoleon produced "the most magnificent sword I ever beheld". The sheath was mostly of tortoise shell studded with golden bees. The handle was of gold, exquisitely wrought. Then she remembered an incident that morning when the emperor's conduct had piqued her, and she instantly determined to punish him for it.

She drew the blade out of its sheath quickly, and flourished it over his head, making passes at him. He retreated until he was pinned up in a corner of the room. She kept telling him she was going to kill him, and he had better say his prayers. "My exulting cries at last brought my sister to Napoleon's assistance. She scolded me violently, and said she would inform my father if I did not instantly desist."

However, Betsy laughed and held her stance, until her arm dropped from sheer exhaustion. Then "Napoleon took hold of my nose, which he pulled heartily but quite in fun; his good humour never left him during the whole scene." (It was Napoleon's habit to tweak her ear, affectionately, but she had had her ears pierced that vey morning.)

An account of this episode appeared in a London newspaper, courtesy of someone in Napoleon's entourage, and then there were different versions of it that appeared in other newspapers: after thinking for a moment that it was a joke, he became fearful and hid behind an armchair, and cried out to his attendants to come to his aid. Las Cases reproached her, but she replied that Napoleon really liked it and asserted, "He loves me! He never really loved anyone, it is not in his nature."

Some people have suggested there was romance between the two, and others suggested that she was mad: "the wildest little girl I have ever met". But the description that seems most apt is that she was extroverted and unselfconscious, and a few years short of being a woman who was eligible for romance.

Betsy's memoir contains many more such exploits, all evidencing the same childlike exuberance and mutual understanding on the part of Betsy and Napoleon. William Balcombe wrote to his patron, Sir Thomas Tyrwitt, to report on Napoleon: "He is very affable and pleasant, plays at cards with us and speaks French with my daughters, amuses himself about the garden and appears in very good spirits."

Napoleon also enjoyed the company of Betsy's two younger brothers, Thomas and Alexander (William was at boarding school in England). Alexander was the same age as Napoleon's own son, back in Europe. He would call them his "little pages", and they sat on his knee and played with his orders (insignia of rank). He asked his staff to make toys for the boys, and he played games with them.

When Napoleon left for Longwood after three months, the opportunity for such interaction was lessened, but they continued to enjoy each other's company when possible. Betsy's father was often at Longwood on account of his duties as the provisioner for Napoleon and his entourage, and the Balcombes occasionally had dinner with him.

A significant change on the island occurred when a new Governor, Sir Hudson Lowe, arrived in April 1816. Napoleon was already unhappy with the situation, complaining that the house at Longwood was damp, the valley was cold, wet and windy, the roof leaked, and there were rats. But Lowe felt that his mission was to be strict, and suspicious of everyone, and the atmosphere between himself and Napoleon was instantly antagonistic.

Napoleon was confined to a space of "about three miles" in which he could walk or ride without encountering a military officer. Beyond that he was required to be accompanied by a British captain. Passes needed to be obtained by anyone wanting to visit. Betsy said in her book that Napoleon's health and activity began to decline soon after his arrival at Longwood. His disputes with the governor did not help.

At one point, when he was endeavouring to learn English, Napoleon sent for some English books, and one of them was an edition of Aesop's Fables. Showing Betsy, he pointed to the picture of an ass kicking a sick lion, and he remarked in English, "It is me and your Governor (Sir Hudson Lowe)".

There were occasionally social events on the island, such as balls, and horse races. The horses were not of high quality, but the event afforded much enjoyment to the people. It is known that Napoleon used to watch the races from a distance, with a telescope. One year, Betsy's pony was not available, and Napoleon (incognito) sent down his quietest horse for her to ride in the Ladies Race, the grey *Mameluke*. It was complete with Madame Bertrand's (from the French party) side-saddle and housings of crimson and gold. Miss Balcombe subsequently won the race.

It then became known that Napoleon was the owner of the horse, and it was the talk of the racetrack. Governor Hudson Lowe was not impressed, and William Balcombe was severely censured and almost dismissed from the purveyorship.

This anecdote comes from Dame Mabel Brookes' book, *St Helena Story*. She goes on to say, Betsy was so upset by Lowe's actions that she went straight to speak with him. Ignoring all protocol, she burst into his office and told him her father had nothing to do with the loan of the horse. Dame Mabel commented, "Betsy may have been a tom-boy, but she also had spirit and a sense of right and wrong... What a brave young lady to face such a man as Lowe!"

In time, some of Napoleon's party left the island. General Gourgaud left, Las Cases left.

The French made numerous complaints against Sir Hudson Lowe and his treatment of Bonaparte. For his part, Lowe wrote, in letters to Lord Bathurst, the Colonial Secretary, in London, his impressions of William. He considered he was "indiscreet, rather than a designing man, liberal, and even profuse. He was living apparently a good deal beyond his means, keeping literally open house."

But Lowe was most concerned about Balcombe's closeness to Napoleon, and suspected he was acting as an intermediary with correspondence to France, and in obtaining monies.

A letter came to William from Sir Thomas Tyrwhitt warning him that his actions were under review. He even recommended that he send his family home. William realised that it would be prudent to depart. He requested six months' leave of absence on the grounds that his wife was ill; the "too warm climate of St Helena" was to blame. In her book, this is the reason Betsy gives for the voyage. She doesn't enter into the political undercurrents of the environment affecting her father.

William would also have been aware that his two daughters were heading towards the time when they needed to be exposed to 'society' and find suitable husbands who had their own income. Governor Lowe agreed to William's request. His position was notionally kept open for twelve months, but Lowe was swift in appointing a replacement for him.

There was a final meeting between Napoleon, William and the two daughters, Jane and Betsy. There were affairs between Napoleon and William that the girls were not privy to; William had indeed been assisting in Napoleon's financial affairs beyond the purview of his official role as provisioner, despite Lowe's intrusive surveillance. The emperor asked Balcombe to visit his family, and made a monetary gift to him for the favour.

Subsequently, Napoleon wrote to William: "I fear that your resignation of your employment in this island is caused by the quarrels and annoyance drawn upon you by the relations established between your family and Longwood, in consequence of the hospitality which you showed me on my first arrival in St Helena. I would not wish you ever to regret having known me."

Part 4: The aftermath of the St Helena days

The Balcombes left St Helena on the ship *Winchelsea,* which was carrying tea from China. They arrived back in London in May 1818. William was still under suspicion, despite Thomas Tyrwitt's support, and Lowe furthered the suspicion with a lengthy letter to Lord Bathurst shortly after the Balcombe's return. At the worst, William Balcombe could have been charged with treason.

The Balcombe family returned to Devon, to William's roots, but the cloud of suspicion remained; William was not appointed to another role, and he had lost his profitable business on St Helena. His financial position deteriorated. But William was never charged with any offences.

Napoleon continued to deteriorate, and he died in May 1821 at Longwood, after a sudden severe illness, at the age of fifty-two. The cause of his death was stomach cancer: not poison, as is still suggested in some contemporary histories. (The medical experts seem to agree.) He was buried on the island, at a spot under willow trees not far from Longwood House. A procession of military and naval officers followed the corpse. In 1840, the British government gave permission for Napoleon's remains to be returned to France. In December 1840, a state funeral was held in Paris with nearly a million attendees.

There was eventually a reconciliation between William Balcombe and Sir Hudson Lowe. Both men were politically prudent. In 1823, William received a new appointment: Colonial Treasurer of New South Wales.

In the meantime, Betsy had grown into a beautiful young woman. Already, at St Helena, she had matured into a young lady much admired among the military and naval officers, and more than one had been suggested as a suitable husband. Back in England, aged twenty, she met a man described as an "extremely handsome man-about-town", Edward Abell. He was supposedly connected with aristocracy, but his parents were of modest means. He was a former army officer on service with the East India Company in India (apparently an undistinguished career), and eleven years her senior.

They were married in May 1822 at Exminster in Devon. Anne Whitehead (2015) asserts (with evidence) that Betsy was four or five months pregnant at the time. The Balcombes went to France to live, to the coastal town of Saint-Omer. Partly this was because William did not yet have a position, and living in France was cheaper, and partly it was because they did not want Betsy's child to be born in England, which would provide evidence that she was much advanced in pregnancy when she got married.

Edward Abell accompanied the family to France. The baby, a girl, was born there, probably in early September 1822 (according to Anne Whitehead). She was later baptised Elizabeth Jane in London, and her common name became Bessie. The marriage with Edward Abell did not last. He abandoned Betsy soon after the baby was born, a serious blow for a young woman in the society of that time. He later said that he had never loved her, and had only married her in hope of gaining some good through her father and his connections.

The laws at this time were solidly patriarchal. Divorce was extremely difficult, and also extremely expensive. It was also the case that if the wife did manage to establish herself independently, with assets and income, the husband could return at any time and take it all. It was his legal right as the husband. He could then leave again. Thus, it was going to be difficult, and risky, for Betsy to survive alone.

It was around October 1823 that William Balcombe was informed that he had been appointed to the new role of Colonial Treasurer in New South Wales. He took his wife and children with him. Given her unfortunate position in England, Betsy and baby Bessie joined them. They sailed on the ship *Hibernia*, a five-month voyage, and arrived in Sydney in April 1824. Unfortunately, the eldest daughter Jane died at sea, off the coast of Africa.

The family had a large, two-storey brick house rented for them by the government in O'Connell Street, and William was assigned six servants. There were few instructions about the job of Colonial Treasurer, and he had to take on many different duties regarding fees, other sources of revenue, and payments. His home had to double as his office and, there being no safe, monies were often kept in his bedroom.

The colony was in transition from being solely a convict colony to being a colony of free people who could develop the complexity and stability of the economy. There were landholders, government employees, convicts who were still serving their sentences, along with convicts who had completed their sentences (emancipists), and free settlers. The government collected revenue through import duties, royalties on timber and coal, wharf taxes and fees on shipping, tolls on roads and bridges, and a variety of other fees.

The revenue was spent on public works, gaols, the police force, the orphan institutions, official salaries, and rewards for services. William's experience at St Helena suited him to his new position in many ways, although it was a much larger challenge. Fortunately, he had been given an assistant who, although young, was very competent.

Balcombe himself was a bit loose with his handling of the funds, and he was known to arrange loans for himself and friends. He quickly became part of Sydney's social life. To add spice to the situation, Betsy had lost none of her allure. In the background, there were also stories from St Helena about William and about Betsy that circulated in the town, so that people made up their own minds about the character of the man, and his daughter. She was deemed mysterious and glamorous, and was referred to on occasion as "the interesting Mrs Abell".

William was also the recipient of land grants, as was customary at the time for government officials. He was given 2,560 acres at Bungonia, south of Goulburn, and he purchased 4,000 acres on the Molonglo River, near Queanbeyan. His son William, just twenty, managed the properties, with the help of assigned labourers, mostly ex-convicts.

William (senior) was continually afflicted with gout, which went back to his days at St Helena, and eventually he succumbed to this and dysentery, in 1829, at the age of fifty-one. He had not had time to consolidate his properties and his finances, and he left his family with debts and with no means of income, although there were still the land grants. The words of Hudson Lowe come to mind, from the St Helena days: "he was generally considered as an indiscreet, rather than a designing man, liberal, and even profuse. He was living apparently a good deal beyond his means, keeping literally open house."

Jane, his widow, went back to London with Betsy to try to obtain a pension. She was unsuccessful in doing so. She obtained a gratuity of 250 pounds, which did little more than enable her to return to New South Wales. She did receive the promise of land, and government posts for her children. Betsy and her brother William took up a land grant at Molonglo that adjoined the original land grant. William lived there for a few years; Betsy for a short time.

However, Betsy was drawn back to Europe. While she was in London with her mother in 1832, she had met with Joseph Bonaparte, the older brother of Napoleon, who had recently returned from America, where he had been in exile. Joseph praised Betsy's "really exquisite and remarkable beauty", and he gave her a cameo ring said to be from Egypt.

Betsy and Bessie went back to England in 1834, along with Betsy's mother, Jane, who was not well. Jane went to live with her sister in Yorkshire, and she died there. Betsy supported herself in London by giving music lessons. Bessie was discovered to be an excellent soprano. Sometimes there would be a visit from French people who had been with Napoleon on St Helena, wanting to refresh their memories of that time.

Betsy published her memoir of St Helena in 1844 with a London publisher, John Murray: *Recollections of the*

Emperor Napoleon on the island of St Helena. It was very popular, and made her instantly famous. There was a second edition in 1853, and a third, produced by her daughter, in 1873.

One of Betsy's visitors was Prince Louis Napoleon, a nephew of Napoleon, who was in London after failed attempts to overthrow the Bourbons from the French throne. He returned to Paris after the revolution in 1848 when he was elected President of the Second Republic. In 1852 he declared himself to be Emperor Napoleon III. He offered Betsy a favour, and she requested a land grant in Algeria, which he granted, but it seems that she never took it up.

Betsy died in London on 29 June 1871, at 6 Victoria Square, in poor circumstances. Her daughter was living with her.

The daughter Bessie had married Charles Johnstone in 1848. He was from a distinguished family and it seemed to be a marriage of love. But they had no children, and Charles died in 1868, so his estate passed to his brother, under the patriarchal laws of the time. Moreover, the brother was not prepared to help Bessie. She went to live with her mother, and life was difficult. Betsy's youngest brother Alexander had offered them a place to live at The Briars in the colony of Victoria, but it was too far for Betsy to contemplate now.

Bessie lived to 1892. She died at St George Hanover Square, London.

Betsy's brothers, the three boys, all remained in Australia. They experienced various troubles. Thomas was initially retained as a survey draughtsman for the Surveyor General. Alexander had already been dismissed from the Commissariat for negligence, and he went to Victoria to take up farming there. William went to the Turon goldfields near Sofala (and Bathurst) in 1844 and died there.

Thomas had an accident in his teens, falling from a horse, and he subsequently had periodic mental problems, culminating in his shooting himself in the head in 1861 at his house (called Napoleon Cottage) in Sydney.

Alexander, the youngest, settled on the Mornington Peninsula in Victoria in 1846. He built an extensive house which he later named The Briars. This was the man who had been but a boy of four when Napoleon arrived at St Helena, and he had sat on his knee. He married Emma Juana Reid and they had nine children. Of these, the youngest was Alice Mabel Maude, who married Harry Emmerton, the solicitor. Their daughter was Mabel Balcombe, who married Norman Brookes, Australia's first international tennis player.

As Dame Mabel Brookes, she had a lifelong interest in Betsy, her grandfather's older sister. She collected many items related to Napoleon, adding to those Betsy had been given by him, collecting items that other members of the family held, and gathering more items from France and around the world.

The collection includes a lock of Napoleon's hair (given to Betsy), a copy of the death mask that was made of Napoleon when he died, which was sent to Betsy by his family in France, branches from the willow tree over Napoleon's grave at St Helena, crockery of Napoleon's, a guitar that he gave to Betsy, plaques and busts, paintings and etchings.

Dame Mabel wrote her own book about the relationship between Betsy and Napoleon: *St Helena Story* (1961). In her will, she bequeathed the whole collection of Napoleon memorabilia to the National Gallery of Victoria. It is on permanent exhibition at The Briars in Victoria. The Briars and the land have been given to the National Trust of Australia (Victoria).

In addition, Dame Mabel purchased The Briars on St Helena, along with the Pavilion, and donated them to the

French Government in 1959. She was awarded the Order of the Chevalier de la Legion d'honneur.

Finally, to take stock of the extraordinariness of the encounter between Betsy and Napoleon, one has to consider the stature of Napoleon on the stage of history.

Today, with historical perspective, we speak of the "Age of Napoleon", as a period of time in which western civilisation was fundamentally changed. Historians have marvelled at the fact that, when once he had achieved great military successes, he turned himself immediately to a grand reform of society. His vision was vast, from religion to social class to administrative efficiency.

Napoleon's rise had come quickly in the wake of the French Revolution and its complete disruption of the established order. In the memoirs that he dictated on St Helena, Napoleon said, "I had but one goal: to reunite all, reconcile all, have all hatreds forgotten, bring everyone together, gather together so many divergent elements and compose them anew in one whole: one France and one *Patrie* (motherland: common identity)."

Napoleon was aware that this vision required practicality, as his memoirs indicate: "My true glory lies not in having won forty battles, but that which nothing will efface is my Code Civil, the verbal proceedings of my *Conseil d'Etat*; the collected correspondence with my ministers, in fact, all the good I did as an administrator, as a reorganiser of the vast *familie francaise*."

The lasting legacy of the Age of Napoleon (as Alistair Horne, 2004, declares) is the notion of social equality and the abolition of privilege. He instituted a regime of advancement on merit. He also exemplified the idea of the "self-made man". He was described by Thomas Carlyle as "our last Great Man". He was called "the emperor of the people".

Perhaps, in this context, it was the innocence and aliveness of Betsy that connected with the great man, at the nadir of his fortunes.

Sources

----, 2006, Balcombe Family and "The Briars" Park, Mt Martha, Victoria, pdf, Mornington Peninsula Shire.

Betsy Balcombe, 1873 (1844), Recollections of the Emperor Napoleon: During the First Three Years of His Captivity on the Island of St. Helena : Including the Time of His Residence at Her Father's House, "The Briars", third edition, John Murray Press, London. (Google Books.)

(Note: Betsy's book was republished in 2005 in hardcover, with the title: *To Befriend an Emperor*, Ravenhall Books.)

Dame Mabel Brookes, 1961, *St Helena Story*, Dodd, Mead & Co.

David Chandler, 1978, *Napoleon*, Leo Cooper, Barnsley, Yorkshire.

Alistair Horne, 2004, *The Age of Napoleon*, Weidenfeld & Nicolson, London.

Rosebery, Archibald Philip Primrose, Earl of, 1900, *Napoleon: The last phase*. Arthur L. Humphreys, London.

Ros Stirling, 'The Briars: an encounter with the emperor, *Australian Heritage*, issue 6, Autumn 2007, pp. 15-19.

Brian Unwin, 2010, Terrible Exile: The Last Days of Napoleon on St Helena, I.B. Tauris.

Anne Whitehead, 2015, *Betsy and the Emperor*, Allen & Unwin, Sydney.

Image 6.1: Portrait of Betsy Balcombe, ~1822 (Brookes, 1961)

Image 6.2: Napoleon with Betsy and Jane Balcombe; Count Las Cases is at left. (Stirling, 2007)

Image 6.3: "The Briars", St Helena (from Betsy's memoir, 1844, p. 17)

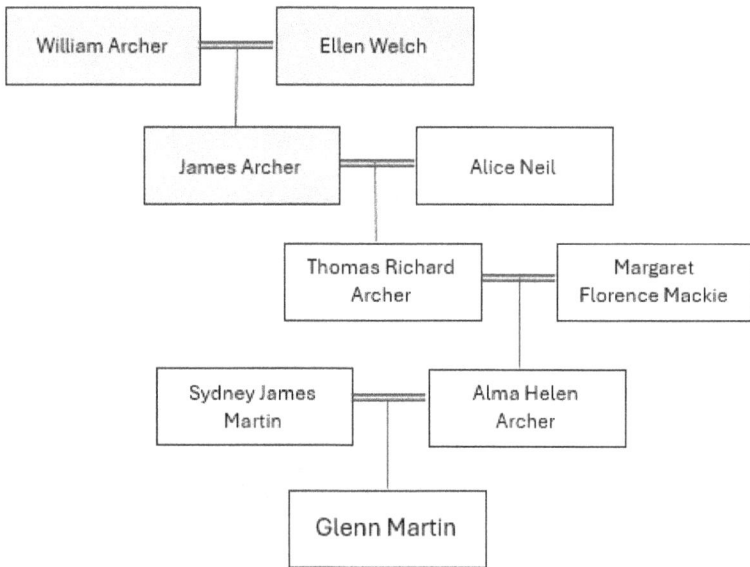

Image 6.4: Chart 1 of 5: the family links from Glenn Martin to Betsy Balcombe. The shaded boxes carry over to the next chart.

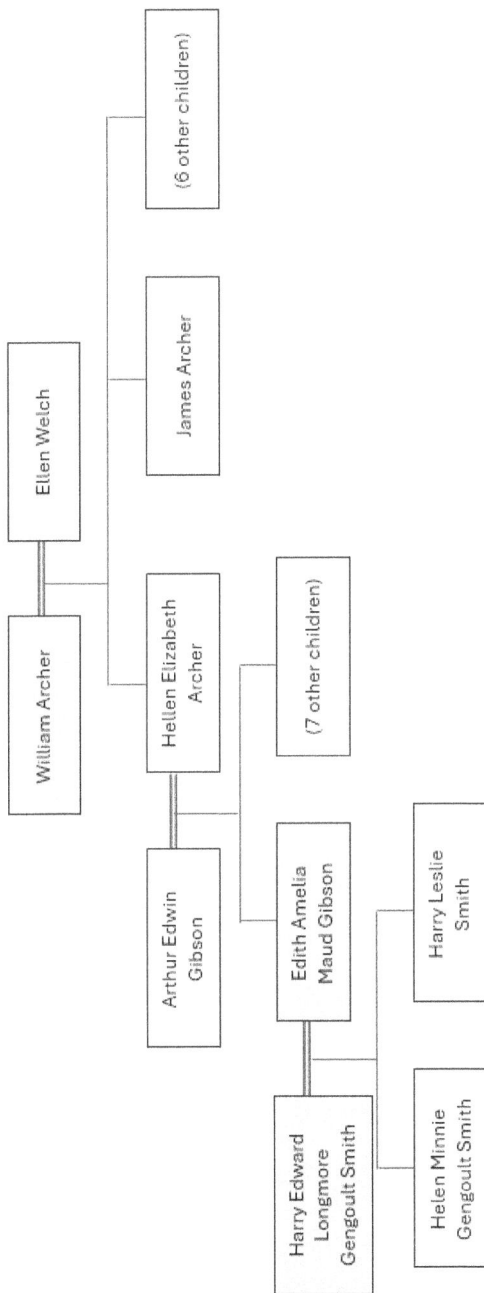

Image 6.5: Chart 2 of 5: from William and Ellen Archer to Harry Gengoult-Smith

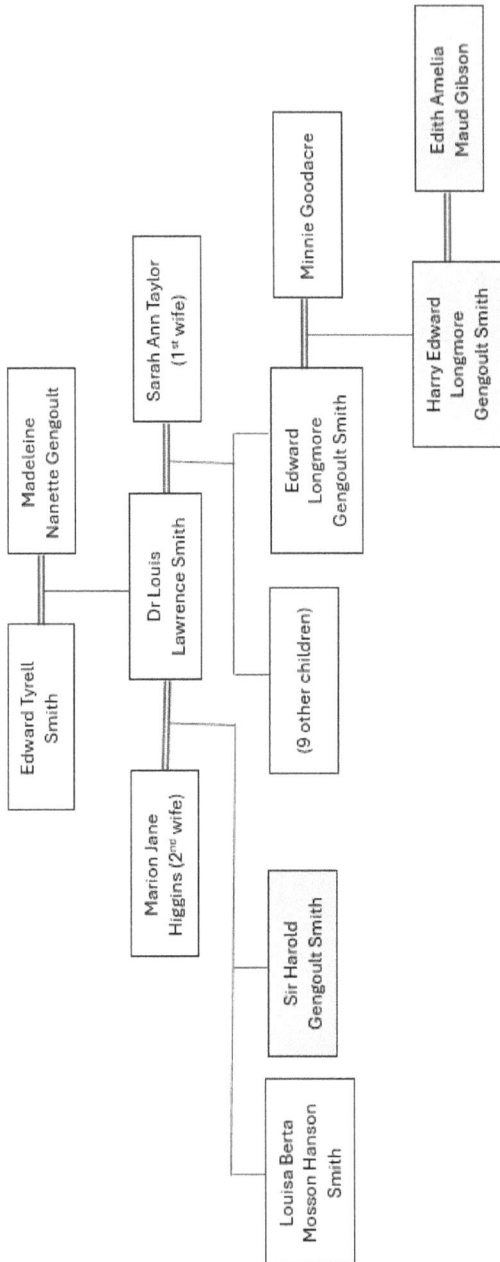

Image 6.6: Chart 3 of 5: from Harry Gengoult-Smith to Sir Harold Gengoult-Smith

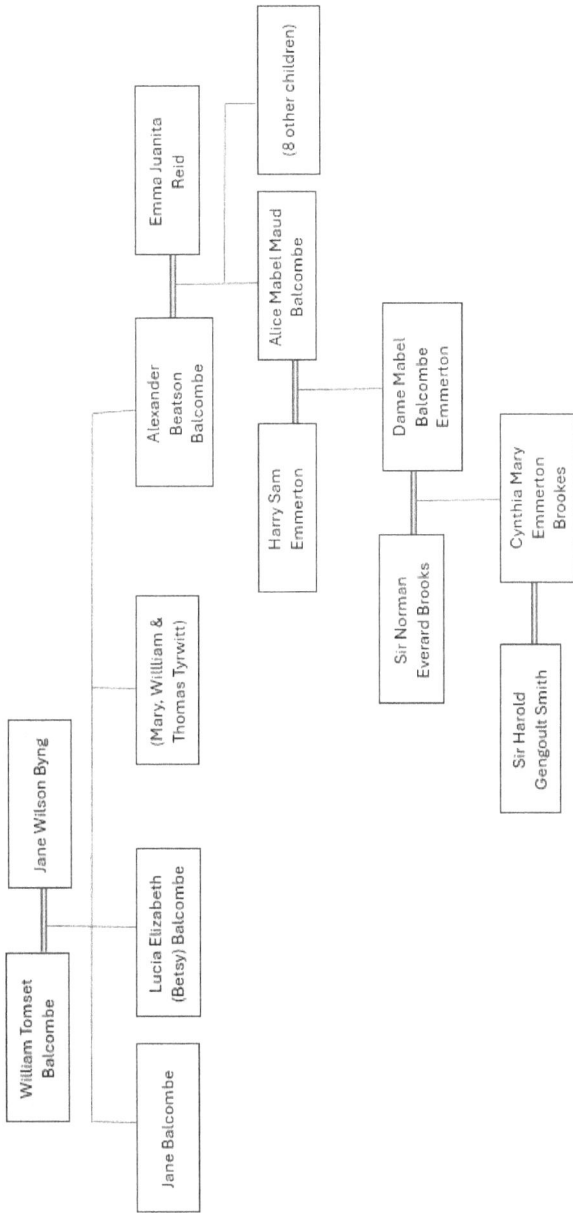

Image 6.7: Chart 4 of 5: from Sir Harold Gengoult-Smith to Betsy Balcombe

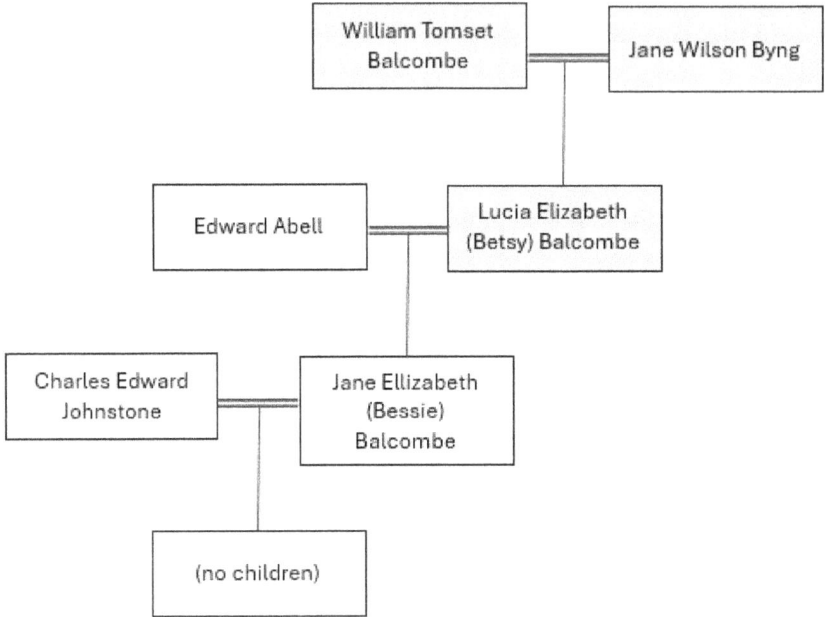

Image 6.8: Chart 5 of 5: Betsy Balcombe, her parents, and her child

7 Thomas Martin: mining manager

Thomas Martin (1834-1904) was my great great grandfather. He was born in Cornwall, was married in 1854, and he emigrated to South Australia in 1857. After gaining extensive experience in goldmining around Victoria, he became the manager of a goldmine at Bethanga, northern Victoria, in 1876, and he held that position until late in life. He is buried at nearby Chiltern.

I knew nothing about my ancestors until I started exploring my family history later in life. Discovering that my father had an ancestry that went back to Cornwall and to mining as a vocation was a huge surprise.

I did a presentation about Thomas Martin for a conference on the Australian goldrushes conducted by the Society for Australian Genealogists in August 2024. Thomas had been involved in the goldrushes in Victoria, but not in the way that I understood most people were involved. My image of the Australian goldrushes was of people abandoning their jobs and rushing off to the goldfields in the hope of finding instant riches. They were shopkeepers, stockmen, schoolteachers, policemen, sailors and clerks. They had no relevant skills or knowledge for goldmining, they just had the sudden feverish desire to get rich, to find a huge gold nugget that would mean they would never have to work again for the rest of their lives.

Thomas Martin, in contrast, came from a long line of miners – for hundreds, probably thousands, of years. Tin mining began in Cornwall around 4,000 years ago. This was deep-shaft mining, not alluvial mining where dirt is washed around in pans with water in a creek, as was most common with the speculators. Cornish miners had always managed to obtain a living from mining – steady, reliable, hard, but sufficient, and seemingly with a level of contentment.

There is a book called *A Poor Man's Diggings*, written by June Philipp, who was born in Bethanga, the place where Thomas Martin ended up.[102] What she highlights is that the Cornish miners had a way of life that was based on community. It would be incorrect to describe them as capitalists, or even as small-time capitalists. Certainly, their enterprise was different to the opportunistic speculators, because it required capital to dig shafts and process the ore they obtained. However, their sense of community was the predominant feature.

The term "poor man's diggings" was used in the latter half of the nineteenth century to refer to settlements where returns were low but steady. It was not a pejorative term; it reflected a positive view of the reliability of the returns. The social aspect was characterised by a spirit of self-sufficiency, independence and egalitarianism. Dignity and self-respect were prized. Poor man's diggings were not big enough to attract a massive rush of people, and usually the means of working the ground involved a minimum of equipment. Susan Lawrence talks about a locality called Dollys Creek, 60 kilometres west of Melbourne, where this description applied.[103]

Bethanga shared these same characteristics, but married it with the establishment of companies which required investment, large-scale equipment, and the readiness to wait for returns. This was a reflection of the Cornish origins of many of the people who flocked to the

---

[102] Philipp, June, 1987, A Poor Man's Diggings: Mining and Community at Bethanga, Victoria, 1875-1912, Hyland House, Melbourne.
[103] Susan Lawrence, 'Poor man's diggings: subsistence mining in the nineteenth century', *Australasian Historical Archaeology*, 1995, 13, 59-68.

places where gold had been discovered. They flocked to Bethanga in 1876. They did not expect great wealth; they hoped for a steady income and a stable way of life.

Why did Thomas Martin leave Cornwall? Many Cornish people went overseas in the 1800s, looking for new endeavours. Many went to America, but in the 1840s, gold was discovered in New South Wales, and copper was discovered in South Australia. In 1846 (when Thomas was twelve), Sir Roderick Murchison gave a lecture in Penzance, urging local tin miners to migrate to New South Wales "and there obtain gold from ancient alluvia".[104] As a youth, Thomas Martin must have been familiar with this talk going on around him, and seen neighbours join the exodus to foreign countries.

Thomas was born in 1834.[105] His home was Chyangweal in Towednack, a few miles south of St Ives, which is on the northern coast of Cornwall. He was the third child. The times were changing, and steam engines were being used to run machinery, especially pumps. It meant you could pump much more water out of the mine shafts, so you could dig deeper, much deeper. And there was machinery to crush the tin ore and copper ore, so you could process much more material.

When an engine was brought to the local mine, Thomas volunteered to man it. He learned the skills, and he was called an engine worker. This job was also called a stationery engine worker or sometimes, simply, engineer.

---

[104] Hill, David, *The Gold Rush*, William Heinemann, Sydney, 2010, p. 25.
[105] Baptism of Thomas Martins, baptised 27 April 1834, Chyangweal, Towednack, Co. Cornwall, 592/1834.

Thomas married Mary Ann Willliams in May 1854 (when he was twenty) and they lived in St Ives.[106] Their first son (my great grandfather) was born in Street-An-Garrow in 1856.[107] (I visited there in 2018. It looked as if it had looked much the same in the 1850s.)

The son was named Thomas, according to tradition: first son, father's name, just as it had been for at least four generations.

These were difficult years in Cornwall. Mining had come upon tough times, because of competition from new mines in overseas colonies. In addition, the British government was promoting emigration to Australia. It ran advertisements in newspapers and put up posters.

Thomas and Mary Ann made the decision to go to Australia. They went as assisted migrants, on the *Carnatic*, a sailing ship of 632 tons, departing from Plymouth in January 1857 and arriving at Port Adelaide in April.[108] The names of all the passengers were published in the newspaper (the *South Australian Register*), so Thomas and Mary Ann Martin were listed, and even the baby Thomas.[109] Note, their name is changed from Martins to Martin. I am not sure why or how this change occurred, but it dates permanently from this time.

---

[106] Marriage certificate of Thomas Martins and Mary Ann Williams, married 13 May 1854, district of Penzance, Co. Cornwall, General Registry Office, England, vol 5c, p 614.

[107] Birth registration of Thomas Martins, born 13 May 1856, St Ives, Penzance, Co. Cornwall, General Registry Office, England, vol 5c, p 346.

[108] Passenger list entries for Thomas Martin and family, Carnatic, arriving Adelaide 28 April 1857 from Plymouth, Archives of South Australia, Passenger lists, 1845-1940, Carnatic, 5/1857.

[109] Shipping Intelligence, 29 April 1857, *South Australian Register*, p. 2. Retrieved January 23, 2025, from http://nla.gov.au/nla.news-article49765092

One would expect that Thomas went immediately to Burra Burra (now called Burra), the place where copper had been recently discovered, and where Cornish families were congregating. Thomas, along with many of the other passengers on board the *Carnatic*, was a miner from Cornwall. But he did not go to Burra Burra. Instead, he stayed in Adelaide and "built a large flour mill and established and carried on a brisk and flourishing business".[110] This was noted in his obituary.

But large finds of gold had been discovered in Victoria in 1851, and Thomas would have heard stories from Cornish men on their way back from Victoria, often with gold in hand, coming back to visit family and to restock for another expedition to the goldfields. The practice was that parties of Cornish men, maybe six or so, would stock up and leave the copper fields at Burra Burra to go to a goldfield in Victoria. They would go for a fixed period of time, maybe 6 – 8 weeks, and then come back. Sometimes they took their family with them.

Sometimes they would come back empty-handed, but mostly they found good-enough amounts of gold to justify their expeditions. Often, they used the money to buy land.

I think that once Thomas heard about the goldrushes, the old Cornish mining sentiments would have kicked in. If there was mining going on, then as a Cornish man he should be part of it, because all of those lifetimes of experience lay there, waiting to be awakened back to life by a new challenge. I suspect he thought that he would do well at it. He left the business in Adelaide, took Mary Ann and young Thomas with him, and went to Forest Creek in Victoria (near present-day Castlemaine).

---

[110] Death of Mr. T. Martin, 30 April 1904, *Ovens and Murray Advertiser* (Beechworth, Vic.), p. 12. Retrieved January 23, 2025, from http://nla.gov.au/nla.news-article199680657

To add spice to the situation, Mary Ann was pregnant, and she gave birth to a daughter, Martha Ann, on 6 September 1858.[111] On the birth certificate, Thomas's occupation is "Engineer". I take this to mean a generalisation of his mining experience in Cornwall to his running of the mill in Adelaide. He chose not to describe himself as a miller or a miner. Rather, he focused on the mechanical aspects of his work.

I think it also showed where Thomas's mind was heading. He was thinking of the running of a mine; he wasn't simply digging for gold. But he was still young. He needed more experience. He needed to know about different kinds of ore and different methods of extracting gold and other minerals from quartz.

Two years later he was at Chapel Hill, one of the many smaller goldfields in Victoria. He had his family with him. Suddenly, Mary Ann got sick. The medical historians say that diphtheria first spread across the world in 1856-58, identified as a new disease, although it had probably first appeared at least a century earlier. It could devastate a family in a week. Usually it was the children who died, but in this case it was Mary Ann who succumbed. She died on 8 May 1860.[112]

Her death certificate said she had had the disease for only two days. Young Thomas was four years old; Martha Ann was poignantly described as "1 year 11 months" old. This time, Thomas was described as a miner (he had come full circle). He would have been devastated. It was a sudden death, and it left him with two young children to look after.

---

[111] Birth registration of Martha Ann Martin, born 6 September 1858, Forest Creek, Castlemaine, Victoria, Births, Deaths & Marriages Registry, Victoria, 18834/1858.
[112] Death registration of Mary Ann Martin, died 8 May 1860, Chapel Hill, Victoria, Births, Deaths & Marriages Registry, Victoria, 6583/1860.

I suppose he could have decided to go home to Cornwall, but he didn't.

At Fryers Creek today there is an "engine house" called the Duke of Cornwall, built by Cornish miners in 1869. It was a gathering place for people from Cornwall. Here, Thomas found himself among familiar people, carrying out a familiar activity in a familiar way. The Rowe family who owned the mine came from Camborne in Cornwall, about fifteen miles to the east of St Ives.

Thomas wasn't quite ready to settle down in one place yet. Somehow, he managed to look after his two children – one assumes that his Cornish kinship was a major factor in this, with women in the community willing to help. I suspect they caught the whiff of his dreaming and wanted to do what they could to enable him.

He travelled to other goldfields in Victoria, and he travelled to Beechworth. We know for certain that he went to Beechworth, because on 4 April 1863 he married Jane Elvira McCartin there, the daughter of a carrier.[113] At twenty-four, she was five years younger than him, and Irish, from Armagh. Thomas and Jane's marriage produced five children to accompany Thomas and Martha: John William, Paul, Eliza Jane, Mabel, and Theresa Elvira.

It was probably in Beechworth that Thomas met a businessman called J.A. Wallace, who owned a hotel there. Wallace was interested in gold mining as a business, while Thomas had acquired extensive knowledge of how to extract gold from quartz, from his Cornwall past and his Australian ventures. They became associates.

Thomas travelled to the various quartz reefs in northern Victoria and southern New South Wales. I think he saw it as his mission, to understand the geology. Over the

[113] Marriage registration of Thomas Martin and Jane Elvira McCartin, married 4 April 1863 at Beechworth, Victoria, Births, Deaths & Marriages Registry, Victoria, 1478/1863.

years 1863 to 1878, Thomas spent time at Barrambogie, near Chiltern, Golden Bay in Victoria, and Hawksview and Yarrara (near Germanton, now Holbrook) in New South Wales.[114] In fact, two of Thomas and Jane's children were born at Hawksview, in 1873 and 1874.

A news article from 1894 talked about Hawksview. A prospector had found gold, but the history of the area was that despite some rich patches, there were no continuous reefs that could be reliably mined for profit. The article says: "Some time ago Hawksview was worked by several Albury syndicates, but the claims were eventually abandoned as being unprofitable."[115]

I suspect that Thomas Martin and J.A. Wallace were one of those syndicates. The article included a story that gives you some idea of the rich possibilities that hovered about: "Several phenomenally rich lodes and leads were struck here (Hawksview), as much as £190 worth of gold being obtained from one bucket of dirt." One tends to forget this in the midst of all the tales of disappointment and hardship on the goldfields. So I think: never forget the dream that drives people onwards.

On New Year's Day, 1876, a valuable new reef of gold, along with some copper, was discovered at Bethanga. It quickly brought hundreds of people to the district, perhaps a thousand, and the majority of them were Cornish. An indication of the predominance of Cornish people among the population is that, in 1878, a public meeting was held to propose building a Wesleyan Church – not Church of England or any other denomination.

---

[114] Death of Mr. T. Martin, 30 April 1904, *Ovens and Murray Advertiser* (Beechworth, Vic.), p. 12. Retrieved January 23, 2025, from http://nla.gov.au/nla.news-article199680657
[115] The discovery at Hawksview, 21 May 1894, *Bathurst Free Press and Mining Journal*, p. 2. Retrieved January 23, 2025, from http://nla.gov.au/nla.news-article62959078

In the wake of this discovery, J.A. Wallace set up a company to establish a deep-shaft mine and extraction plant, and Thomas Martin became the mine manager. It can be said that the drivers for Martin and Wallace were different. Thomas Martin's goal was sustainable yield, an ongoing business. Wallace wanted a quick hit that would give him wealth and fame. He was an entrepreneur, who later became a member of the Victorian Parliament.

By 1878, the two children that Thomas had with Mary Ann had grown up. Martha Ann was twenty, and she got married in May 1878, in Albury. Thomas, the son, got married in January 1879, aged twenty-three. What was significant about this marriage was that Thomas married a girl from Cornwall, Philippa Dower, and that the marriage was in Bethanga, where both Thomas the son and Thomas the father were to spend the next twenty-five years. Philippa's parents were also living in Bethanga. Her father, William Dower, was likewise a miner, from Crowan, which was just south of Camborne.

Of the mining community, June Philipp said: "The gold miners who came to Bethanga in the latter 1870s were men for whom prospecting and gold mining were a subsistence way of life that had become habitual. Few gold miners held illusions about what might be in store for them." They were working people, and they soon became aware that Wallace was an aggressive entrepreneur. He was deceitful and manipulative. In 1885 the miners formed a branch of the Amalgamated Miners' Association of Australasia. Note, the main attraction of the union was not wages and conditions, but benefits in the case of injury. Injuries were not uncommon. But the existence of the union led to conflict with Wallace and a lockout.

The miners were exasperated with Wallace, and they picketed the smelting works all one night. Philipp reports that the women turned up as well, "turning the scene into quite a moonlight picnic". It was a night "that could have turned ugly"; "instead, it became a time of gaiety and celebration; fires were lit, refreshments served all round, and momentarily at least, community was re-established".

Wallace saw that only defeat and vengeance remained, and peace was re-established. The rhetoric of class warfare did not enter into the dispute. The quarrel of the Bethanga miners was with Wallace, and it was intensely personal.

But Philipp says: "Wallace's aims at Bethanga were complex.... Bethanga represented a challenge that he found irresistible; he would conquer Bethanga's ore and he was determined that victory, when it came, would be personal, complete and spectacular. To that end he was prepared to sacrifice his own money, the interests of his shareholders, and the well-being of the miners and the town."

The difficulty the company faced was that although gold and copper were present, the process for extracting the minerals from the quartz was not working efficiently enough. Advice was sought from mining engineers from around the world: France, Germany, America and Great Britain.

Many thousands of pounds were spent on experiments and equipment, but the problem had not been solved, and it looked as if the company would have to close the mine, which had not yet returned a dividend to the shareholders. Some of the attempts also set the townspeople against the mine, because they involved burning the ore for a month in open heaps, generating choking fumes that blanketed the town. The mining and smelting works, which had employed about 150 men, were effectively closed for several years; until the mid-1890s, employment was reduced to a maximum of thirty.

Throughout the 1880s the Martins – it is not always possible to distinguish Thomas Martin senior from his son of the same name – continued at work trying to solve the problems of the 'bears' that formed in the blast furnace or convertor. At the end of December 1887, the Mining Registrar declared that Martin had solved the problem at last.

Philipp comments that Wallace was attempting to bring off a miracle at Bethanga, and he had become attached to the idea of himself as a legendary character. Thomas Martin – and his son's, approach was that success lay with the careful selection of ore, gradual improvements to the smelting works, and the appropriate use of the chlorination process.

A recent account by the Federal Department of the Environment, which was looking at the historical significance of the mining site and processing plant, describes what happened next: "Having spent more than 10 years trawling the globe for experts to (find a viable extraction process), Wallace's problem was finally solved by his own works manager".

The account says that Thomas Martin knew the Bethanga ore better than anybody. He focused on one of the older processes, but made a number of modifications to it, and the furnaces were rebuilt as well.[116]

The revised process was successful, and the Bethanga mine became profitable, both for copper and for gold. By 1895, the Wallace Bethanga Company had attracted a takeover bid, and Bethanga Goldfields Limited was formed, with Thomas Martin being appointed the first chairman of directors. He held this position for almost ten years, until his failing health forced him to relinquish the position.

The gold gradually petered out, and the goldfield had ceased operations by 1912. In the meantime, Thomas Martin

---

[116] "Wallace Smelting Works, Martins Road, Bethanga, Victoria"; www.environment.gov.au

the younger had taken up a position as mine manager at nearby Chiltern. It was called the Lady Rose goldmine, but it was never a great success. This Thomas Martin moved away, coming up to Sydney with his family around 1915 (preceded by some of his children) when the mine closed, and he started a new life as an engineer.

An obituary for Thomas Martin the elder was published in *The Wodonga and Towong Sentinel*, Friday 6 May 1904.[117] It starts: "Deceased was a native of St. Ives, Cornwall, England, and landed at Adelaide in 1857."

The article says he was known as "the father of Bethanga" for his role in establishing the Bethanga gold fields. Thomas often said that solving the problem of extracting the ore, and establishing a viable mine, was the dream of his life. As well as being noted on the Department of Environment's heritage listing, Thomas Martin's innovations are discussed in a PhD thesis by Ralph Winter Birrell.[118]

But it was not just his engineering prowess for which Thomas Martin was respected. He was also seen as an outstanding manager, and one who cared for the people around him. To quote the obituary article again: "Frequently, in the absence of a medical man, was he called out to set a broken limb or advise in the case of an illness, and many a one has occasion to remember, with gratitude, his kindnesses in these and other directions."

The *Sentinel* had published an earlier article about the death of Thomas Martin on 29 April in which it said, "He was a man of unimpeachable integrity, indomitable

---

[117] The late Mr Thomas Martin, 6 May 1904, *Wodonga and Towong Sentinel*, p. 3. Retrieved January 24, 2025, from http://nla.gov.au/nla.news-article69544961
[118] Ralph Winter Birrell, University of Melbourne, 2005, "The Development of Mining Technology in Australia, 1801 – 1945", PhD thesis.

perseverance, and of a most charitable disposition, never hearing a tale of distress without doing his best, unobtrusively and unostentatiously, to relieve the sufferer. His efforts in this direction were recognised by the committees of the various charitable institutions. He was a life governor of the Ovens District Hospital, Ovens Benevolent Asylum, and Albury Hospital. He also rendered very valuable service to the Roman Catholic Church, Bethanga. Mr Martin was an honorary magistrate, in which capacity his ruling principle was to temper justice with mercy."[119]

On a visit to Bethanga in October 2024, I found a booklet in a package of historical materials which was kept at the hotel. It was a short history of the local Roman Catholic church. Thomas Martin was mentioned. Before any churches had been built, his house had been the venue for church services for both the Methodist and Catholic Churches.[120] (He was Methodist, being Cornish, but his wife was Catholic, being Irish.) It seemed fitting that he would be so broad-minded despite the common antipathy between church denominations in that era.

Thomas Martin was buried at Chiltern, where he had lived towards the end of his life. I have a photograph I took of the headstone on his grave. I think it is amazing. This is what it says:

By the Employees of the Bethanga Goldfields Co Ltd. To the memory of Thomas Martin, their late manager who laboured among them for 25 years and earned the respect and goodwill of all. Born at St Ives, Cornwall, England. Died aged 70 years. We loved him.

---

[119] Death of Mr Thomas Martin J.P., 29 April 1904, *Wodonga and Towong Sentinel*, p. 3. Retrieved January 24, 2025, from http://nla.gov.au/nla.news-article69544918
[120] P.R. Packer, 1992, A History of St Francis, Bethanga.

I have never read anything like this on a headstone. It is a message from a whole community, far beyond family, and it is a message of utmost respect. Thinking of those last three words: "We loved him": I think of the world we live in, just over 100 years later, and I try to imagine a group of employees formulating a message to go on the headstone of their recently deceased manager's grave. It is difficult to think of any manager about whom the words, "We loved him" would spring to mind.

Yet what Thomas Martin did, and the person that he was, do not seem beyond the reach of ordinary people. He was intelligent, to be sure, and determined, and he respected and cared for those who worked for him. None of this is superhuman. But then, I think, he did this for a lifetime; it was not a charade. It was an admirable life.

The Cornish people were important in mining across Victoria. While visiting Daylesford in 2022, I came across a cairn that had been erected for Cornish pioneers, and it specifically refers to deep quartz mining in the area by Cornish folk.

June Philipp ends her book, *A Poor Man's Diggings*, with these words: "This history is a salute to all those men and women who created the community of a poor man's diggings and shared its life.... With the odds stacked heavily against them they tried, and briefly succeeded, to realise an ideal very different to that lived by Wallace and symbolised and celebrated in his legend. The community that was fashioned from a poor man's diggings was outwardly crude and ramshackle but not brutal. Its achievement, which in the modern world has been peculiarly elusive, was a community built on mutual trust."

* * * * *

My other stories about Thomas Martin are contained in two other books I have written:

- A Modest Quest (2017) and
- *All the Rivers Come Together* (2022) ("The long journey to fulfilment")

There is also a video presentation at
https://youtu.be/4BocZgT1giA

Image 7.1: Left: Thomas Martin (b. 1834), ~1895 (Chiltern Museum),. **Right:** Gravestone of Thomas Martin (d. 1904) at Chiltern (Author)

Image 7.2: Mining at Upper Bethanga, 1906 (Philipp, 1987, p. 146)

8 The coalminer's daughter: Ellen Welch from Balgonie Furnace

Part 1: My great great grandmother's story

Ellen Welch is my great great grandmother: my mother's father's father's mother. She was the wife of William Archer, who came to Australia as a convict in 1838 (on the ship *Waterloo*), and who later in life established the Duke of Edinburgh Hotel in Pyrmont (Sydney) and was the publican there. William was born in the town of Harpenden, Hertfordshire, England in 1813.

Ellen was born in the town of Balgonie, Fife, Scotland in 1822. She came to Australia in 1841 on the ship *New York Packet* as a single, female, assisted migrant. Her passage was paid for under the colonial government's bounty system. She went to the Hunter Valley as a domestic servant and met William. They married and spent their lives together.

I wondered why Ellen emigrated. She was the fifth of six children; she was the only member of the family to emigrate. Everyone else: her parents and her siblings, stayed in Fife, in the vicinity of Balgonie. Her father was the manager (or grieve) of a coalworks (coalmine) at Balgonie Furnace (near Markinch). She was the youngest of three girls; they were the boss's daughters.

However, her death certificate says she was born in Edinburgh, and the birth certificates of her children say the same about her. This does not align with the fact that her birth certificate (about which I am certain) shows that she was born at Balgonie Furnace This was odd. Was there something to hide?

I obtained her Unmarried Female Immigrant certificate, signed in Sydney on 23 October 1841. Her character and person are vouched for by two gentlemen in Edinburgh. The certificate says she was born in Dublin. There were other Irish women on the migrant ship, but none from Dublin. I think Dublin is not true; I am satisfied she was born in Fife, as Helen Welsh. I think the claim about Dublin was a clumsy form of camouflage. (Besides, she would have had a Scottish accent!)

Note that the spelling of names in the records of this time was not always consistent. A switch from Welch to Welsh (or even Walsh) and back again did not necessarily signify anything of import. It might simply mean a name was written down phonetically, or the writer was mistaken or careless.

Ellen had been in Edinburgh, as seen from the immigration certificate, but she had also been in Glasgow, as the ship departed from Greenock, which was nearby. As luck would have it, the first British Census was conducted on 6 June 1841, not long before Ellen's ship left for Australia (on 8 July).

The Census shows Ellen Welch, aged twenty (the age is not quite correct, but the convention in this census was to round ages off to 20, 25, 30 etc.), in a boarding house in Glasgow, and she was with a one-year-old boy, Thomas Welch. Ellen's correct age was eighteen; she turned nineteen during the voyage. I also looked for 'Helen' and 'Welsh' and 'Walsh'; there were no competing persons. Nor was there an Ellen, or Helen, Welch/Welsh anywhere in Fife, or elsewhere in Scotland, that could have been her.

I think that she altered her name slightly when she went through the process of emigrating as an assisted migrant. Her name in the Census is the same as her name on the immigration certificate, so I think this was something of concern to her, and to which she gave her attention.

The question is, how could she have a child living with her in Glasgow in June, and then board the migrant ship four weeks later alone, as a single woman? What happened to the child?

I have to guess. The Roman Catholic Church had started an orphanage in Glasgow in 1832 after a typhoid outbreak. Many adults had died, and there had been a rise in the number of orphaned children. I think that Ellen took the child to the orphanage and gave him to the nuns. It is a stunning story.

We can assume the child was hers, but who was the father? And why did she feel she had to leave home – irrevocably? To give up the child was extreme.

In Australia, Ellen married William, and they had eight children. The first four were named after William and people in his family. The next three children were named after people in Ellen's family (but not her father). The last child was called Thomas, which did not correspond to names in either of their families. Ellen had not forgotten him.

There is still the question of who the father of the child was, and why she felt she had to leave home. She was probably sixteen when she became pregnant. My idea is, she was the boss's daughter, as the songs say – a particular source of attraction for men. And was her father one of those severe, religious Scots who would have been outraged if he found out his daughter was pregnant?

Part 2: The coal industry in Balgonie

Alexander Welch was the manager of the coalmine at Balgonie Furnace. But first, we have to talk about coal in Scotland. Coal was first mined in Scotland in the late 1200s, when the Abbot of Dunfermline was given authority to work surface outcrops of coal in Pittencrieff Glen. The coal was not sold commercially, but given out to parishioners for domestic fuel.

Coal may be found exposed on the sides of valleys and glens, and sometimes on the surface. The first miners hacked into these outcrops. The use of coal was initially limited by the difficulty of transporting it over distance. The roads between centres of habitation could better be described as rough tracks than as roads.

The coal most likely to be mined was near the coast, where ships could be brought in close and loaded up. Many of the coal-heughs (a steep bank containing coal) bordering the Firth of Forth were able to get comparatively large cargoes away by sea.

Demand for coal was also stimulated by the growing scarcity of timber, despite Acts of Parliament ordering the holders of land to plant and preserve trees, and imposing severe penalties on the destroyers of "green wood". Moreover, over time, coal was being used more and more for industrial purposes. In the early 1700s, windmills were introduced to drain mines of water. A number of windmills were set up in Fife, probably due to the prevalence of winds along the Firth of Forth.

The first major coal-using industry in Fife was salt evaporation. Boiling sea water to make salt was a huge industry and a vital part of the Scottish economy. It flourished where coal was found close to the sea. The water was boiled in large rectangular iron salt pans which were set up in special pan houses at various places around the coast. (There are the remnants of a saltworks and a windmill at St Monance.)

At the beginning of the 16th century, the annual output of coal in Scotland probably did not exceed 40,000 tons, and as this output came from places as far apart as East Fife and South Ayrshire, most of the collieries were probably part-time concerns. Coal working was on a small-scale.

Initially, the collieries were run by the monasteries that controlled much of Scotland's land and wealth, but after the Reformation of 1560 they came under the control of big landowners who sought to work them for a profit.

John and Alexander Landale, who leased Balgonie coal from the 5th Earl of Leven, in 1732 made use of both water wheels and a windmill for drainage. The latter was equipped with 8-inch pumps to raise water from 14 fathoms (a fathom is six feet, or 1.8 metres, a measure principally used for depths such as in water or mines). However, the mine was undersold from the early 1740s by the neighbouring county.

The invention which, far more than any other, contributed to the rapid expansion of industry was due to the genius of James Watt. By 1784 Watt had so far perfected his double-acting, rotary steam engine that it could be employed to drive machinery of all kinds. The age of steam power had arrived, and the Industrial Revolution had begun. The steam engine meant a new lease of life for coal. Steam power was now available to deal with the age-long menace of mine waters, and to raise water, and coal, from greater depths than had been previously possible; underground workings could be extended and new fields of coal opened up.

The next major development was the application of steam-power to the "travelling engine", as the first locomotives were called. This led to a boom in railway construction, beginning around 1830. In the 19th century, the constant challenge to the coal industry was to match the demands of industrialisation. Scotland's annual production of coal rose from 1.6 million tons at the end of the 18th century to about 17 million tons by 1873.

Despite the acceleration caused by industrialisation, during the 19th century Fife's mines remained relatively small. Most of what was mined was exported from small harbours like West Wemyss. However, in the last quarter of the 19th century, mining in Fife suddenly became a major industry, an event that coincided with the rapid expansion of rail and sea transport. Both needed coal, and Fife coal was ideal, and as well as burning it themselves, steam ships and locomotives carried coal to markets at home and abroad.

Balgonie Colliery sank a new shaft, the Lochtyside Pit, in 1846. It operated as a pumping shaft, using a Cornish beam engine, and the No. 9 shaft was used for ventilation. In 1883, a new shaft, the Julian Pit, was sunk. The shaft reached the Dysart main seam at 80 fathoms, and coal working started in 1885. The colliery was worked as part of the Balfour family's Balgonie and Balfour Estates operated by the Balgonie Colliery Company, a concern in which the entire shareholding was held by the family.

By the late 19th century, coal had become a vital part of everyday life in Scotland, providing fuel for homes, gasworks, iron and steel works, electricity power stations, railway locomotives, ships, and thousands of mills and factories. Coal reached its peak production in 1913, just prior to World War I. At this time, all industries had one major factor in common – they were totally dependent either directly or indirectly upon coal as their principal source of energy and illumination.

The Scottish coal industry employed almost 150,000 people, and accounted for approximately 15% of annual British coal output. The coals were generally of a high quality, and suitable for a range of uses within Scottish industry.

Although the early decades of the 20th century saw a relative decline and stagnation in the industry, an optimistic mood prevailed after World War II. In 1947, nationalisation took the coal industry into the care of the state, and there was a genuine belief that working conditions and economic performance would be greatly improved.

In the 1980s the industry was re-privatised, in the Thatcher years, following which Scotland's last deep mine was closed permanently in 2002.

The modern incarnation of the Balgonie Colliery commenced in 1883, and it was worked until 1960. Its average workforce was 448, with the peak workforce being 490 in 1952. There were two working shafts, 147 metres deep and 119 metres deep. The average output was 470 tons per day.

In the Markinch parish, there are two villages and an estate. Balgonie proper, or Milton of Balgonie, stands on the left bank of the river Leven, east of Markinch rail station. Coalton of Balgonie village stands south of Markinch. The ancient mansion, Balgonie Castle, likewise stands on the banks of the Leven. The title of Baron Balgonie (created in 1641) was still borne by the Earls of Leven in 1885.

The Rev. Mr. John Thomson gave an account of Balgonie and its coal mines in 1791. He states that Balgonie coal, the property of the Earl of Leven, was discovered and wrought from as long ago as 1500, and perhaps even 1300. In 1517 the Coaltown of Balgonie is mentioned in a scheme of division and valuation of the county of Fife. Rev. Thomson observes that coal waste could be traced for upwards of three miles, indicating a long period of mining. The mining was not continual; there were long periods when no mining took place.

In 1731, "it was again set a-going by Alexander Earl of Leven, who erected a water engine, which wrought two sets of pumps, with 9-inch working barrels, and which dried the coal to the depth of 30 fathoms. In the year 1732, this coal was let to tacksmen, who carried it on for some years (until around 1743), but meeting with large hitches yielding much water, their engine was overpowered." (Rev. Thomson)

The Balgonie Colliery was re-erected around 1785 (reported in the Statistical Account of Scotland for the parish of Markinch in 1791). It resulted in a considerable increase in the population. The parish of Markinch at this time had two large collieries: Balgonie and Balbirnie. The output of Balgonie in 1791 was averaging 30 tons per day. Consumption of coal was increasing, and demand was great.

Yet, predictions in 1791 about the future of the mine were constrained: "how long the field may last, it is hard to say, though it is scarce possible, allowing the quality to be good through the whole extent of the known field, that any coal will remain to work 50 years hence."

There is no doubt that people had come to rely on coal. An extract from the Statistical Accounts of Fife 1791-99 for the parish of Monimail states: "... Coals chiefly from Balgonie and Balbirnie, in the parish of Markinch, at 7d per load, of 18 stone, are the fuel of the parish. A double cart carries five loads; the carriage costs nearly the purchase in money. ..." And the same was true in 1836: "The fuel principally used is coal, brought from the parishes of Markinch and Dysart. ..."

In 1823 Balgonie estate, having belonged to the Earls of Leven from the reign of Charles I, was purchased by James Balfour. The records show that the coal grieve (mine supervisor) in 1823 was Mr Alexander Welch, Ellen's father. In 1842 the average number of colliers employed at Balgonie and Balbirnie Collieries was thirty.

With more powerful engines now in use, predictions about the future of the mine were more optimistic: "With more powerful engines for drawing off the water, the coal seams at Balgonie may be regarded as inexhaustible."

Part 3: Alexander Welch

The ancestors of Alexander Welch (1780-1860), going back at least as far as the 1600s, came from the vicinity of Balgonie. His grandfather came from the Coaltown of Wemyss, as did his father, and Alexander himself. Alexander died at Markinch in 1860. The Census of 1851 describes him as an annuitant (at age 70; an annuitant is someone who is entitled to regular payments of a pension). One can safely assume that this pension related to his career with the Balgonie Coalmine as the grieve.

Baron F. Duckham (1970) describes the various roles that began to be differentiated at coal mines in the 1700s. Most of these roles were operational, such as the gatesmen who kept the roadways within the coalmine free, and the onsetter who hooked up the batches of coal to go up to the surface.

And then there were some roles pertaining to supervision and management of the mine overall. Often, the mine owner played an active role in the management of the mine. This was the case with the Balfour family, who had taken over the mine in 1823. However, the growing workforce required the supervision of men fulfilling various operational roles, and a competent and honest grieve was critical to the mine's smooth functioning.

The coal grieve is a coal miner or person employed in a coal mine who is in charge of management, supervision and administration of coal production and work. The word 'grieve' comes from Middle English, and means steward or overseer.

The fact that Alexander Welch was kept on as grieve after the Balfour family took over, and worked through to his retirement, suggests that he was indeed a competent and honest grieve. It was not the case that all men who worked in the mines were competent or of upright character.

Duckham says that the recruitment of grieves tended to favour following the family line. If a father held a role, especially a management role, it was hoped a son would follow in the same line. I believe this was the case with Alexander, and that the family tradition as grieves had been established before he grew up. Duckham says that high status was attached to the role "in an industry only slowly emerging from serf and near-serf labour" (the statement relates to around 1800).

Duckham also says, "There was a strong religious aspect to the function of the grieves, although most did not live up to it. Not all people were competent in their roles." He quotes Lord Dundonald, who "cursed oversmen, who to a considerable share of gallantry with the colliers' wives and daughters, add the further qualifications of being notorious drunkards, and the damn'dest scoundrels, in general, under Heaven."

Duckham is suggesting that some of the managerial staff in the mines took liberties with the wives and daughters of the colliers. Thus we come to the idea that Alexander Welch's own daughter may have been subject to the liberties of a coalmine employee. Add to this the likely fact that Alexander Welch was a strict adherent to the church's moral code, and one sees the possibility that when Ellen Welch became pregnant, she felt obliged to flee.

Part 4: The children of Alexander Welch and Helen Forbes

In the 1841 Census, Alexander and his wife Helen were living in the village of Thornton, which is just two miles away from Coaltown of Balgonie. Alexander's occupation is "Manager of Coalworks". Living with them at this point were just two of their children: Elspeth (26, the eldest) and Archibald (15, the youngest).

George, 25, was married to Agnes Dunsyre and living in Wemyss (about five miles from Coaltown of Balgonie, and which also had a coalmine), working as a coalminer. They had three children: Archibald (6), Christian (2) and Agnes (<1).

Alexander, 24 was married to Elspeth Simpson and they had three children, but they are not located in the Census for 1841 or later. They both died in Fife.

Archibald is in the 1861 Census with wife Janet McRae at Wemyss, with five children who are all still living at home. His occupation is Grocer and Miner.

It seems clear that the sons continued in the tradition of coalmining (except for Alexander, who is unaccounted for), although none of them is the manager of a coalworks. However, it should be considered that in the years when the position may have become available, the mine was entering a period of decline.

Alexander, Ellen's father, turned sixty in 1840, and he was still working in the role of manager when the Census occurred in 1841. It was ten years later when the Census showed him as retired.

Balgonie Colliery sank a new shaft in 1846, as a pumping shaft, but it was not until 1883 that a new shaft for hauling up coal, the Julian Pit, was sunk. And the writers who gave an account of the Balgonie mine maintained that mining in Fife remained relatively small until the last quarter of the 19th century, when mining in Fife suddenly became a major industry.

Part 5: William and Ellen in later life

As people migrated to Australia during the 19th century, fractures in families were common. Some families had members who were adept correspondents who kept in touch with their families 'back home', but many families never heard from the emigrants ever again. Ellen could read and write, as indicated on her migration certificate, so writing home was not out of the question, but I think that it did not occur, because of the issue of her becoming pregnant.

I do not know what Ellen's parents knew. Did they have any idea where she went? Did they even know that she had become pregnant? Did someone help Ellen to get away, and support her while she was pregnant? How did Willliam Goodsir, the bootmaker in Edinburgh, come to be involved in the migration?

In the register of immigrants to New South Wales for 1839 to 1851, Ellen's certificate of migration shows that Ellen came to the colony "under the protection of" William Goodsir and his wife. I discovered that he was a bootmaker living in Queens Place in Edinburgh. How that connection was initiated, I do not know. Although, I did discover that William's parents came from Fife. Perhaps someone friendly to Ellen in Fife knew that William and his family were now in Edinburgh.

There are many questions. Did Ellen's father make any attempt to find her or bring her home? Or did he find out her plight and disown her?

While I was researching for another family ancestor, Edward Lewis (another great great grandparent of mine), I came across a Missing Person report for a man of that name. (It turned out not to be my relative.) This Edward Lewis had gone to the Australian colonies, and his family back in England did not know where he was. They hoped that the police could help to locate him, and the police pursued the matter.

The family knew his birth date and place of birth: 24 May 1830 in Northern Shropshire. He went to the colonies on the steamboat *Burra Burra* in 1855, going from Liverpool to Melbourne. His occupations were goldminer, farmer, and publican. He was married and he had a daughter and four sons. He was last heard of in Temora, New South Wales in 1883, but a newspaper article from Sydney in 1887 or 1888 suggested he could be keeping the Mercantile Hotel at 635 George Street.

That was a lot of detail! The Inspector General of Police in Sydney responded to the inquiry to say he had found the person. He had spoken to him, and he had promised to write to his family at an early date.

This was not an uncommon occurrence in Australia's colonial days, and the police were generally helpful. But we do not know if the Welch family even knew that Ellen had gone to the Australian colonies. They certainly would have had nothing like the detail the family had for the Edward Lewis above. At the worst, she could have gone elsewhere in the world, or she could have been somewhere else in Scotland, or she could have been dead.

In my family I have no examples of correspondence between the colony and the family back home. However, many people did write back regularly to explain their circumstances and the nature of their new environment. Some of these letters found their way into newspapers for the information of the broader public.

One example from the *Aberdeen Journal* in March 1840 was a lengthy description of the emigrant's arrival in Adelaide and his subsequent arrival at Port Phillip Bay (Melbourne). He was not impressed with the Adelaide of the time: "The town of Adelaide is one of the most straggling places you could conceive, and the distance from the port is seven or eight miles." Although, he did say that "the country is certainly pretty and much resembles a gentleman's park".

The correspondent was much more complimentary of Port Phillip. He refers to the countryside as Australia Felix, the term used by the explorer Major Thomas Mitchell for the lush pastures in much of Victoria. It reminded the writer of the fine grass at home. He ends by saying, "Had I had room, I would have told you more, but as my letter is almost full, I must have done."

None of this relaxed, expansive talk between family members remained to Ellen or to her family. She was simply gone, and she was gone forever.

There is, however, another chapter in the story. Later in life, William and Ellen Archer did a remarkable thing. In the late 1860s they decided to return to England. William was about 57, and Ellen about 48. They left Australia and moved to Kent, southeast of London. They had several of their children with them. There were older ones who were already married and who did not accompany them.

They purchased a fruit orchard of 3 ¼ acres (1.3 hectares) at Wilmington and lived there for about five years. We know all this from the 1871 British Census.

They were only about twenty miles from London. Did William venture home to Harpenden? Did they venture north to Scotland, to Fife?

William's parents had both died. So had Ellen's. Would William and Ellen have known this? Probably not. However, they both had siblings still living in the neighbourhoods of their youth. Yet, I think these meetings did not occur, and perhaps it was when William and Ellen both realised that all the old bonds were broken, they decided to return to Australia. They returned in December 1874. It was after this that William built the hotel in Pyrmont.

In the 1871 Census, the question is asked, where were you born? The answers given for William and all the children are correct. William says he was born at Harpenden, Hertfordshire. The children were all born at Gloucester (Hunter valley), New South Wales. But what does Ellen say? She says, 'Scotland', but the town is "Not known". So, at the age of forty-eight, she is still hiding the truth.

After their return to Australia, Ellen adopted the name Helen, and it is the name Helen by which she is memorialised on her gravestone. At first I thought this was an act of pretension, as the family was latterly enjoying good fortune. However, Helen was actually her birth name. So, why have I retained her name as Ellen Welch? I suppose it is because this was the name under which she came to

Australia, and the name under which she was married. And also, I have become attached to her story as Ellen Welch.

Part 6: A visit to Markinch

In June 2025, I visited Markinch, as part of a six-week trip to England, Scotland and Ireland. It was my intention to explore facets of my family history as well as to enjoy the various places I visited. At Markinch, I thought I might at least find evidence of the Welch family in the church graveyard.

The church, St Drostan's, is at the top of the town, walking up the hill from the rail station. The church is very old. Its first known form was built prior to 1050. New buildings succeeded it, beginning with one built in the early 1100s built by the MacDuff family. The square tower dates from 1050, while the rest of the church has been remodelled numerous times since.

I was given a tour of the church, which has two levels, one downstairs and one above it, up a wide staircase. Upstairs it was pointed out to me where the Balfour family pews were. They were the important family in the parish, as we have seen in the account of the mining industry.

The Balfours sat in front at one side, looking down to the Minister, while there were pews behind them for their servants, and a private staircase nearby for the use of the family only. The man who had assumed the role of tour guide told me that this tradition had persisted until quite recent years.

In the graveyard outside, in a prominent position, I found the gravestone of Lieutenant-General Robert Balfour, who died 31 October 1837. He was one of many in the Balfour family who held important positions in Scottish and English society over a long period of time. The colliery was only one of their fields of interest.

And yes, in the church records, I did find one family member: Helen Forbes, Alexander Welch's wife, Ellen's mother. She died on 28 November 1854; she was one of the last people to be buried in the graveyard. Her gravestone is no longer standing. After 1854, the deceased were buried in the new graveyard across town, which is still in use. Alexander Welch is buried there; he died on 18 February 1860.

And I met a group of parishioners having morning tea in the church hall across the road from the church itself. As I walked up the hill, in the quiet street I saw a sandwich board saying, "Tea and Coffee". I felt the need for a cup of tea after my travels from St Andrews that morning, so I entered the hall. There was a group of a dozen people, mostly women, seated around a large table with tea and scones.

They welcomed me and asked me where I was from. I said I was from Australia, although it seems that in Scotland I only have to say one word and people tell me I must be from Australia. As I sipped tea and ate a scone, I told them some of Ellen's story. I didn't tell them the whole story, with the pathos of the child left behind in Glasgow, but I told them she had left Markinch at a young age, went to Australia, married a convict from England, and lived in Australia for the rest of her life. I said she was the only one of her family to emigrate, and I didn't know if she ever had contact with her Scottish family ever again.

I felt as if I was bringing her home after more than 180 years. This was the welcoming group. I felt that they understood.

When we had finished tea, two gentlemen in the group said, "We should go over to the parish office now, and we will see if we can find any of Ellen's family in the records." And so I was shown the burial record for Helen Forbes in December 1854. Up to twelve persons of the name

Welch were buried here as well, but there were no individual records for the burials, or gravestones for them.

Sources

Baron Frederick Duckham, 1970, *A History of the Scottish Coal Industry, Vol. 1, 1700-1815, A Social and Industrial History*, David & Charles Newton Abbot.

Guthrie Hutton, 1999, *Fife: The Mining Kingdom*, Stenlake Publishing.

National Coal Board, 1958, *A Short History of the Scottish Coal-Mining Industry*, National Coal Board, Scottish Division.

Miles K. Oglethorpe, 2006, *Scottish Collieries: An Inventory of the Scottish Coal Industry in the Nationalised Era*, Royal Commission on the Ancient & Historical Monuments of Scotland.

Website: Fifepits.co.uk

Image 8.1: *New York Packet* ship, built 1837, England (MIT Museum)

Image 8.2: Gravestone for Helen Archer, died 1912, Waverley Cemetery, Sydney (Author)

In loving memory of Helen, beloved wife of William Archer. Died 8 June 1912, aged 89 years.

Not a sound disturbs your slumbers
Not a care to mark your brow;
All your pains and trials are over
You are happy resting now.

9 The Romance: An old story and an older one

In my book, *All the Rivers Come Together* (ARCT, 2022) there is a story about a romance that I heard from my mother, a story that I concluded was invented by William Archer and his wife, Ellen Welch, my great great grandparents. The story is simple: A boy (who is English) is working as a groom at a royal castle. He meets a girl (who is Scottish) who is also working at the castle, as a maid. They fall in love, get married, save up their pennies, move to Australia, and establish a hotel at Pyrmont, Sydney.

Once I embarked on family history, in my sixties, I discovered fault lines between the story and reality. The last part of the story is definitely true: William Archer, who came from England, did establish a hotel at Pyrmont, called the Duke of Edinburgh, in the 1880s. It is still in existence, although it is now called the Harlequin Inn. And William was married to a Scottish wife, Ellen Welch. But they did not meet in a castle, and in any case, how does an English lad meet a Scottish lass in a royal castle?

William was a convict when they met, transported for theft in 1838; he was working off his sentence on a farm in the Hunter valley north of Sydney. Ellen had come to Australia as an unmarried female migrant, assisted under a government scheme. She went to the Hunter valley as a servant. And yes, they met, married, and had children.

The story I told in ARCT addressed the question: where did the story come from? And I concluded that they, William and Ellen, had made it up. The story camouflaged the fact that he had been a convict, and it was a nice story to tell the children. So, the story passed on down until it got to my mother, who once again passed it on. I was happy with this explanation; it seemed quite possibly true, and it fitted in with my feelings about the kind of people that I thought William and Ellen were.

However, after a while I felt a niggle. Yes, my story might be true, but what if there was something more to it? What more could there be? I thought that it must have to do with Scotland. Ellen came to Australia from Scotland alone. No one else in the Welch family came. And my mother also had other Scottish ancestry, the Mackie family, and she certainly regarded herself as being part-Scottish. For example, she knew the Mackie tartan.

She was the daughter of Margaret Florence Mackie, who married Thomas Richard Archer, a grandson of William Archer, and Margaret was a descendant of an entire (Mackie) family that had come out from Scotland in 1852.

My new question was, could there have been a story in this Scottish line that was subsequently fitted together with the story that William and Ellen Archer had made up? Imagine this: Thomas says to Margaret, "This is a story that has come down through my family." And he tells her about the groom and the maid, the castle, and the two people falling in love, getting married and coming to Australia.

And in response, Margaret says, "I've got a love story too." What is it that she tells him?

She tells him this story. There was a boy, and he grew up in the Scottish countryside. It was at Kilconquhar in Fife. There was no castle there, but there was the next best thing: a great house that had guests, servants, grounds and everything grand. So the boy, Robert Bridges (born 1719), worked at the great house. He may have even worked as a groom, looking after the horses. But he grew restless, and wanted to run away and see distant places.

And he did. He ran away to Edinburgh. He was thinking that he would join the throng of Scots who were going to the New World: America and Canada. But in

Edinburgh, because he had worked at the great house at Kilconquhar, he found it easy to get a job at Edinburgh Castle, which is a royal castle. And he started an apprenticeship there as a baker.

Meanwhile there was a girl, one Margaret Richy. She was born southwest of Glasgow at a little place called Lochwinnoch in Renfrewshire, in 1725. She also had the desire to see what life was like elsewhere. Perhaps there was also trouble at home that caused her to leave. We don't know.

Margaret ended up in Edinburgh, and she found a job as a maid at Edinburgh Castle. Thus, she met Robert. And one thing they had in common was that they had both left home, and home was a long way away.

Their love blossomed, and they decided to get married. They found a minister in Edinburgh, William Jamison, who performed the ceremony for them on 8th April 1748. He gave them a signed certificate of marriage, which would be helpful to them if they needed to show anyone that they were indeed married.

It must have been tempting for Robert and Margaret to consider embarking for the new world, and perhaps they discussed it, but eventually they decided to go back to Robert's home territory: Fife. Robert had learned his trade as a baker at the castle: he was now called a Journeyman-Baxter (which means a baker who has finished his apprenticeship, and who has acquired skills and experience in the trade), so he would find work wherever he went, and his family had lived in Fife for two generations.

However, there was a problem once they returned to Fife. The Church of Scotland was powerful in the community, and it had an important say in how people lived their lives. Robert and Margaret were living in the parish of St Andrews and St Leonards, near to the city of St Andrews. From the parish committee's perspective, Robert Bridges had arrived in the community with an unknown woman, and they were living together as man and wife. This was irregular and unacceptable.

The parish committee called a meeting (on 8th June 1749), and summoned Robert and Margaret to appear before them. The couple were interrogated and asked to explain themselves. But Robert was ready for this occasion. He produced the paper signed by William Jamison, Minister, which he called his "marriage lines".

The committee were not happy with this turn of events. They rebuked the couple for their "irregular marriage". One might note that the church did not claim that the marriage was non-existent or invalid, and it did not require the couple to remarry. Instead, the couple were "taken bound to live together as man and wife". However, Robert was made to feel obliged to make a payment to the church in order to settle things down.

He "gave his Bill for five pounds as Scots payable against Martinmass next, to pay to the Clerk and Beddall's dues". ("Martinmass" is a date in the church calendar; the "Beddall" was an officer of the church dating back to the Middle Ages, an administrative role, also known as a Beadle. These words are taken from the Clerk's account of the committee meeting, all recorded in a book of the proceedings of the council in tidy handwriting.)

I was curious as to how much five pounds was worth in 1749. I learned that a teacher's annual salary in the county around that time was 34 pounds, so we could say, roughly, that five pounds was two to three months of Robert's wages – quite a lot.

Robert and Margaret had four children (a fifth child died as a baby). They lived in Fife all their lives, although they moved away from the parish of St Andrews and St Leonards to the village of Anstruther Easter, further down the coastline of Fife. Three generations later, a descendant, Rachel Bridges, and her husband Alexander Mackie, left

Scotland for Australia, taking their whole family (five children still living at home) with them.

*   *   *   *   *

Both of these stories feature two young people who meet while working in a royal castle. They fall in love and get married. There is distance involved. In one story, the two get together and then decide to emigrate to Australia. In the other story, the two people meet after travelling a long distance, and then they go back to the hometown of one of them.

In the first story, the couple do a remarkable thing: they go to Australia and establish a successful hotel. In the second story, the couple also do a remarkable thing: they go back to Fife and win acceptance from the local community (after making a generous donation to the church).

In both cases, the couple has a vision of the future that extends beyond the local community, and it is held together by the love between the two people.

I wonder about how the story of Robert Bridges and Margaret Richy was translated into a story that could be told to their children and their children's children. Perhaps it was the beginning of their story that was lent to the story's later version: there was a boy who worked in a royal castle, and there was a girl who worked there too, and they met and fell in love. Then they married and had adventures, and settled down happily with their children.

*   *   *   *   *

I think about this for a while, and I wonder if I have some of it wrong. Why would I think this? Because: what if it wasn't William and Ellen who made up the part of the story with the royal castle in it? After all, the royal castle belongs to Robert Bridges and Margaret Richy's story. And if so, then the story of the romance and the royal castle must have come down the Bridges-Mackie family line and was eventually told by Margaret Florence Mackie to her husband Thomas Richard Archer. My mother was sure that it was a royal castle, not just any old castle.

And I have another thought. A few years ago, I interviewed an Archer relative, Graeme Brennan. We are both great grandsons of Willliam Archer and Ellen Welch. I told him the story of the romance that my mother had told me, and he hadn't heard it. So, if this is true, it fits with the idea that Thomas Richard Archer and Margaret Florence Mackie were the ones who made the story up and/or passed it on, or at least, put it together in a new way. (Graeme's grandmother, Dolly, was the youngest sister of Thomas Richard, my grandfather.)

$$* \quad * \quad * \quad * \quad *$$

When I had started exploring family history, my first thought about my mother's story was how it compressed time. A boy meets a girl, they fall in love and get married, then they sail to Australia and establish a hotel. Even if the boy and girl had been Willliam and Ellen, and they had really met in a castle somewhere in Britian, forty years actually passed before the hotel was established.

So, I think, it seems that an invented story can compress time. If the story of the romance in the royal castle is true (Robert Bridges and Margaret Richy), then the story compresses generations, because Robert and Margaret lived all their lives in Fife. It was their great granddaughter, Rachel Bridges (that is, three generations later), who set sail for Australia with Alexander Mackie.

Once this point is accepted, then it is easy to add the flourish: they set up a hotel in Sydney. And the proof of the story is in the hotel: it was real (called the Duke of Edinburgh Hotel), and in fact, it still exists, in 2025 (called the Harlequin Inn).

And for us, there is even a joke beneath the surface: the name 'Edinburgh' is in the name of the hotel, evoking 'Edinburgh Castle', even though the name of the hotel really referred to the second son of Queen Victoria who visited Australia in 1875-1876.

(I also think the name of the hotel is a nod to England, given that William Archer came from England (Hertfordshire) and that William, Ellen and children went back to England in the late 1860s and lived in Kent for five years before returning to Australia.)

* * * * *

My conclusion: I think the two stories were too attractive to resist, and they were stitched together by my grandparents, Margaret Florence Mackie and Thomas Richard Archer, to tell their children. This would have been in the period around 1920; they were married in 1910 and my mother was born in 1923. I don't think there was a concept at that time of historically based family history. You either knew nothing, or you had a good yarn to tell. This, of course, pertains to ordinary people, not prominent social identities whose lives are more public.

I certainly think that William Archer was a seasoned raconteur, a man who lived to tell stories from behind the bar. I would happily credit him with the whole story, but I believe there is a strong Scottish element to it, and that only comes when Margaret Florence Mackie marries Thomas Richard Archer.

* * * * *

The background to the whole story is the growing mythology surrounding emigration from Britain to Australia in the 1800s and 1900s.

Although Robert Bridges and Margaret Richy did not emigrate, the mythology of emigration was in the family. The first Bridges person in America was reported to be Clement Briggs, who came to Plymouth, Massachusetts in 1621 (in an account written by Dolorus Briggs, 1960, located on the Family Search website).

A note is necessary about the name Briggs. Dolorus Briggs explained that it derives from Bridges. Some Scots people changed their name from Bridges to Briggs when they went to America. Back in Scotland, this became a fashion too, in evocation of the bold emigrants, and names were often changed from one to the other and back again during a person's life. I have discovered this in my family tree with the names Bridges and Briggs.

I have other instances of people in my family tree changing their surnames upon emigration: Thomas Martins came from Cornwall, and he changed his name to Martin on arrival in Australia, dropping the 's'. John Neill came from the county of Armagh in Ireland, and he dropped one 'l' from his name when he came to Australia (hence Neil).

The latest incidence of the name Briggs in my family occurred with George Briggs Mackie (born 1863, my great grandfather). For a long time, I wondered where the name Briggs had come from. You have to go back three generations to find it. I discovered it came from George's great grandfather, George Wilson Briggs, who was the grandson of our Robert Bridges. Why would you give one of your children the middle name of Briggs unless you were trying to keep the name alive? And why would you do that unless there was some story associated with it?

So, I think there was definitely a story that was passed down, even if the form of the story did not reveal or reflect all the facts.

Nowadays we might rankle at the fact that Robert felt it necessary to pay the church around two months' wages to pacify the church authorities for a concocted misdemeanour. But in the bigger picture, he held his head high, he became a part of the community, and he baked its bread! The spirit of independence was alive in his family, and that spirit eventually took his great grand-daughter, Rachel Bridges, to Australia at the age of forty-five: she, her husband and their whole family.

By the time of their emigration, the power of the church over people's lives had diminished. There was a phrase in the scribe's account I wondered about. The church committee referred to the Minister who signed the marriage lines rather scornfully: "signed by one William Jamison, himself Minister", as if that were a thing that was hardly possible.

After I had read this account, I realised there was another story on the previous page of the book, that dealt with another "irregular marriage". The issue was the same, and a young couple was interrogated in the same way: why are you living together as man and wife when you did not get married in this parish? And this couple did the same thing; they produced a paper as evidence that they had been married by a minister. The account described this as follows: "subscribed by one William Miln, who designs himself Minister. They were rebuked for their Irregularity and taken bound to live together and to behave dutifully towards one another as husband and wife during their lives."

Apparently, some people were 'real' ministers (ie Church of Scotland) while there were dubious others who "design themselves" as ministers. I resorted to an account of the parish of Kilconquhar written in 1837 by the Reverend

William Ferrie. This is close enough in time and place to give us an idea of the religious lay of the land. He says that in the parish of Kilconquhar in his time, there were 2,300 who belonged to the Established Church (the Church of Scotland), and around 360 who were Dissenters of various sorts: the United Associate Synod, the Relief, the Independents, and a few Baptists.

I think the important thing about the intervention of the church in Robert and Margaret's marriage was that it cemented the circumstances of their love and marriage in the family's memory forever. Without the (now) incongruous actions of the church, the circumstances of their meeting might have faded into the past. The parish committee meeting served the purpose of highlighting exactly what the church was disparaging: the love of two people who had met in a distant place, who had asked the blessing of a minister for their bond, and who were now living together faithfully as man and wife.

* * * * *

Sitting behind both of these stories is the perennial theme of how a boy and a girl meet. There is an element of surprise and wonder in the event. Even when the two are born near to each other, there is an element of wonder, that two people can notice and like each other, and want to commit to each other, and for the long term.

Alexander Mackie and Rachel Bridges are a case in point. They were born in Fife, both in 1807, and less than five miles apart: Alexander in Earlsferry and Rachel in St Monance. But is five miles no distance at all, or is it as far as a distant world? Somehow, they met. Both their fathers were fishermen; perhaps this was the connection.

However, near to Earlsferry and St Monance was Kilconquhar House (less than five miles away. The original

128

building was Kilconquhar Castle, going back to the 1200s, when it was held by the Dunbar family. It was rebuilt in the 1500s as a baronial mansion house. This is the same place where I think Robert Bridges worked around 1735. It was sold a number of times until 1764, when it was purchased by the Lindsay family. The current holder of the house and estate is the 16th Earl of Lindsay.

It is not out of the question that Alexander Mackie and Rachel Bridges worked here in the mid-1820s, in such jobs as groom and maid. They were both eighteen in 1825, and the house would have needed staff. I think of it as a parallel to young people today whose first job is at a supermarket. It's work experience, it gives them their first experience of earning money, and it lightens the burden on their families.

They were twenty-five when they got married. In the marriage record, Alexander is from Kilconquhar and Rachel is from St Monance (her birthplace). The marriage was at St Monance. Later (in the 1841 Census), Alexander was a weaver and a stonemason.

"There was a boy, and he worked as a groom in a royal castle. And there was a girl, who also worked in the castle, as a maid. And they met and fell in love, and got married, and then did something remarkable in their lives, all the while loving one another. And there were children...."

Sources

Births, deaths, marriages, and Census data

Scotlands People: https://www.scotlandspeople.gov.uk/

Victoria and New South Wales Births, Deaths and Marriages Registries

Other references

Church council proceedings re marriage of Robert Bridges and Margaret Richy, 1749, National Records of Scotland, Old Parish Registers Marriages 453, St Andrews and St Leonards, pp. 423-424 of 462.

Kilconquhar Parish, description by Rev. William Ferrie, January 1837.

History of the Briggs-Bridge family: since its settlement in America (Virginia) in 1752; with genealogy as found in early church records, government documents, wills and family correspondence, by Dolorus Briggs Mansfield, published by Mrs. W. Sloman, 1960, Pawnee, Illinois. (from Family Search website)

Websites

East Neuk Estates, Kilconquhar:
https://www.eastneukestates.co.uk/about-the-estates-of-the-east-neuk/kilconquhar/

Kilconquhar Castle Estate: https://www.kilconquharcastle.co.uk/

Simon Forder, The Castle Guide:
https://thecastleguide.co.uk/castle/kilconquhar-castle/

Trove.Scot, Kilconquhar House:
https://www.trove.scot/place/32553

Image 9.1: Engraving of Kilconquhar House in its grounds, 1812. Titled 'Kilconquhar House', for *Scots Magazine and Edinburgh Literary Miscellany*, published in Edinburgh by Archibald Constable & Co.

Image 9.2: Edinburgh Castle, 2025 (Author)

10 After completion

This has been a book of stories, nine of them. Obviously, there is a larger context from which the stories have come, and in which more stories are hovering, some already forming, some still unformed, and some still unknown. The stories here were chosen because they attracted my interest. There was something that lifted the arc of the person's life above the ordinary.

The arc of a person's life is like a contest between fire and water. At any stage, the fire can dry out the water completely, or the water can extinguish the fire. One hopes for that sweet spot where the fire heats the water and you can make a nice cup of tea. But life does not often present itself to us that way; there is more generally struggle and confusion. Although the stories here go way back in time, it still matters to me how the people sought to find that sweet point of balance between the fire and water in their lives.

Behind the stories there is a large family tree, and the people here occupy particular places in that tree. Some of them are direct ancestors of mine, and others are a little further removed: cousins, second cousins, cousins of grandmothers. It is easy for particular people to be overlooked, easy for them to be forgotten, yet they all have something worth remembering about their lives, something to offer for our consideration, and they all ask of our sympathy or our admiration. At worst, they give us pause for caution.

And behind the family tree there is an idea, the idea of the family, and what it could be like, and who we are within a family: sons and daughters, brothers and sisters, fathers and mothers. And more: grandsons and granddaughters, and for some of us, grandparents. And we might ask: what is our role, the role that we would desire of ourselves, that we also might deserve admiration, or at least, sympathy?

These are the deeper questions of family history. It is not mere distraction and entertainment.

"Understand the past in order to nourish the future."
Stephen Karcher

Family tree chart: five generations

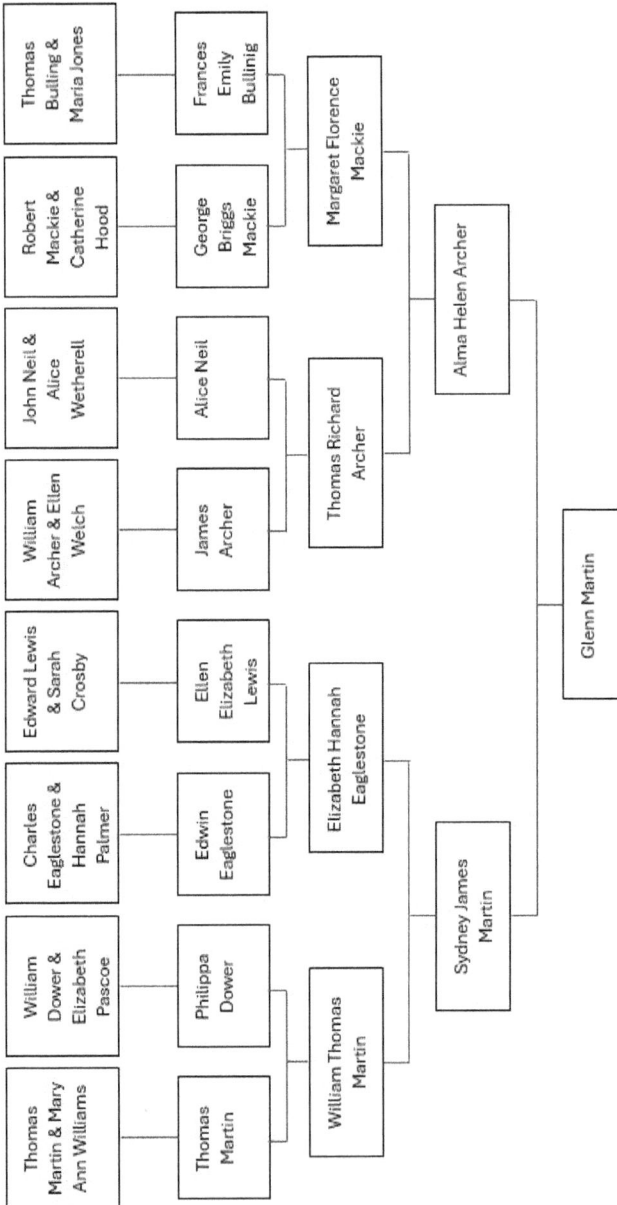

Thomas Martin & Mary Ann Williams	
	Thomas Martin
William Dower & Elizabeth Pascoe	
	Philippa Dower
Charles Eaglestone & Hannah Palmer	
	Edwin Eaglestone
Edward Lewis & Sarah Crosby	
	Ellen Elizabeth Lewis
William Archer & Ellen Welch	
	James Archer
John Neil & Alice Wetherell	
	Alice Neil
Robert Mackie & Catherine Hood	
	George Briggs Mackie
Thomas Budling & Maria Jones	
	Frances Emily Bullinig

William Thomas Martin

Elizabeth Hannah Eaglestone

Thomas Richard Archer

Margaret Florence Mackie

Sydney James Martin

Alma Helen Archer

Glenn Martin

Acknowledgments

I have received assistance from the staff and volunteers of many history and family history organisations, including:

- Hornsby Shire Family History Group
- Royal Australian Historical Society
- Society of Australian Genealogists
- Bath Historical Society
- Oxford Family History Society
- Fife Family History Society, Cupar
- National Archive of Scotland
- National Library of Scotland
- Scottish Genealogical Society
- City Library of Edinburgh
- St Drostan's church community, Markinch

And I also have received help from many individuals, including Gerard Dickinson and Anne Shipley of London, in my exploration of the Archer family in Wilmington.

As well, I have received supportive feedback from friends and family.

Thank you, all.

Author profile

Glenn Martin is the author of over twenty-five books. He is an independent scholar and teacher. He has written on ethics and values, family history, reflections on experience, and he has produced several volumes of poetry. His scattered career includes teaching in high schools and at tertiary level, management of community-sector organisations, writing commentary on employment law and management for professional publications, editing a national magazine for trainers, and designing online education courses. He has graduated from the workforce.

Glenn lives in Sydney. He has also lived in the hills in far northern New South Wales, where he wrote two books of local history. He has five children and four grandchildren.

This is Glenn's seventh book on family history.

Other books by Glenn Martin

Reflections on experience
The Ten Thousand Things (2010)
Sustenance (2011)
To the Bush and Back to Business (2012)
The Big Story Falls Apart (2014)
The Quilt Approach: A Tasmanian Patchwork (2020)
Long Time Approaching: An Incomplete Memoir (2023)
Travel with a Pen (2023)
Library Meets Book Fair (2024)

Books on ethics and values
Human Values and Ethics in the Workplace (2010)
The Little Book of Ethics: A Human Values Approach (2011)
The Concise Book of Ethics (2012)
A Foundation for Living Ethically (2020)

Books on the big picture
Future: The Spiritual Story of Humanity (2020)
A Singular Book of Great Esteem: Life with the I Ching (2025)

Books on family history
A Modest Quest (2017)
The Search for Edward Lewis (2018)
They Went to Australia (2019)
No Gold in Melbourne: A Scottish Family in Australia (2021)
All the Rivers Come Together: Tracing Family (2022)
The Sailor, the Baron and the Dressmaker (2024)

Poetry collections
Flames in the Open (2007)
Love and Armour (2007)
Volume 4: I in the Stream (2017)
Volume 3: That Was Then: The Early Poems Project (2019)
The Way Is Open (2020)

Local history
Places in the Bush: A History of Kyogle Shire (1988)
The Kyogle Public School Centenary Book (1995)

INDEX

Names of ships, titles of books are given in italics.

Darling Harbour (Sydney), 25–27
Dollys Creek (Victoria), 86
Duke of Cornwall ("engine house"), 91
Duke of Edinburgh, 29–30
Duke of Edinburgh Hotel, Brixton (England), 30
Duke of Edinburgh Hotel, Pyrmont, Sydney, 4, 25, 30, 53, 101, 119, 124–125. *See also* "white horse" controversy
Dynnyrne House, Hobart, 19

Eaglestone, Blanche Ellen, 46
Eaglestone, Edwin (great grandfather), 46
Eaglestone, Elizabeth Hannah (grandmother), 46
Eaglestone, Sarah Ellen, 46
Earls of Leven (Scotland), 105, 107–108
Edinburgh (Scotland), 101–102, 112, 120–121
Edinburgh Castle, 121, 125
Elba (island), 61–62
Elm Cottage, 15
emigration. *See* migration
Emmerton, Cynthia Mary, 56
Emmerton, Harry, 57

female convicts, 8, 10, 11, 13, 18–20
Fink, Alice *See* Mackie, Alice
Fink, Best & Hall, 33–34

Fink, Gordon
    Australian Imperial Force (AIF) and war service, 4, 32–40
    birth, 1
    death, 32–33, 38–40
    employment, 2, 3, 32
    Gallipoli, 4, 32, 36–40
    in Victorian Field Artillery, 34
    law studies in Melbourne University, 33
    marriage and annulment, 4, 32–34
    Star, Victory Medal and British War Medal, awards of, 41
Fink, Theodore, 32–33
first world war, 32
Forbes, Helen, 110, 116
Forest Creek (Victoria), 89
Fryers Creek (Victoria), 91

Gallipoli, 4, 32, 36–41
Germany, 1, 47–48
Gibson, Arthur Edwin, 53
Gibson, Edith Amelia Maud, 54–55
Glasgow (Scotland), 102–103, 121
gold, 87, 89–90, 92–93, 94–95
gold miners and mining, 91, 93
goldfields, 85, 89–92, 95–96. See also Australia's gold rushes
Goodsir, William, 112

Hagen (ship), 48

www.ingramcontent.com/pod-product-compliance
Lightning Source LLC
Chambersburg PA
CBHW060350090426
42734CB00011B/2094